YEADON'S REGISTER

of

L N E R

LOCOMOTIVES

Volume Eighteen

**Gresley K1 & K2, Thompson K1/1
& Peppercorn K1**

Copyright Booklaw/Railbus 2000
ISBN 1 899624 46 5

YEADON'S REGISTER OF L.N.E.R. LOCOMOTIVES - VOLUME 18

EDITOR'S NOTE & ACKNOWLEDGEMENTS

The locomotives featured in this volume of Yeadon's Register were designed, built and operated through the three railway steam ages of the British Isles - pre-Group, Grouping and Nationalisation. The Gresley K1 was in fact his first design on joining the Great Northern Railway and his later K2 was so well received it went on to serve not only the GN but the LNER and BR with little change to the original design.

Moving on to the end of the LNER period, into the Thompson era, we come across a single engine, No.3445, which was a rebuild from an earlier Gresley type. The rebuild was classified K1 as first but later became K1/1 so as to leave K1 vacant for the Peppercorn version of that rebuild. The Peppercorn K1 engines, though of LNER parentage, were all delivered during the early years of British Railways and featured many innovations that were then currently in vogue. These seventy engines though short lived compared with the Gresley 2-6-0's were eventually to be amongst the last steam locomotives working on the former LNER lines of BR. They, like the previous K1 and K2 were good mixed traffic engines which, when called upon, could perform virtually any task given them.

In presenting these classes the Register has now finished with all the locomotives covered by the K classification (K3, K4 and K5 classes were the subject of Volume 8) and in subsequent volumes we will obviously see more of those alphabetically classified wheel arrangements 'put to bed'.

Without Eric Fry's continuing enthusiasm and proof reading abilities this volume would probably have not seen 'the light of day' but his somewhat devoted services ensure that what is printed is fact rather than probability. Therefore, it goes without saying that this series has the benefit of not only WBY's superb research but also at the production stage, EVF's expert eye for spotting the occasional gaff before its reaches you the reader.

In the Brymor Jones Library at the University of Hull, Brian Dyson and his patient archive staff have once again been readily available to help with all sorts of requests, even at short notice and the editorial team thank them for their continued support and professionalism. For anyone interested in this series who has not yet visited the archive, it is well worth the trip. Besides the railway archive, there is much to interest the transport historian and enthusiast.

Annie, Jean and Simon, must be thanked for their patience and understanding whilst sitting on the sidelines. Hopefully this, the eighteenth volume of *Yeadon's Register of LNER Locomotives,* will meet their usual approval.

And, once again, not forgetting you the reader, for your continuing support.

The next Register, Volume 19, will feature the GN and M&GN 4-4-0's.

The Yeadon Collection is available for inspection and anyone who wishes to
inspect it should contact:-
The Archivist
Brynmor Jones Library
University of Hull
Hull
HU6 7RX
Tel: 01482-465265
A catalogue of the Yeadon collection is available.

First published in the United Kingdom by
BOOKLAW/RAILBUS 2000 in association with CHALLENGER
309 Mapperley Plains, Nottingham, NG3 5RG.
Printed and bound by The Amadeus Press, Cleckheaton.

INTRODUCTION

GRESLEY K1

A single engine, No.1630, was built by the Great Northern Railway at Doncaster (Works No.1354) in August 1912 as the forerunner of what was to become LNER Class K1. Nine similar engines entered service from Doncaster during a three month period from February to April in the following year. These ten engines were the first 2-6-0 type to built by the GNR besides being Nigel Gresley's first design for the company. They were classified H2, Class H1 covered a batch of American supplied 2-6-0 'kit built' engines purchased by the GN some years previously.

Designed to haul heavy goods trains at fast speeds, the H2 class proved a success and further engines, this time with larger boilers and classified H3 (LNER K2) were built at Doncaster in 1914. Before Grouping two of the Class H2 engines had been rebuilt to H3 and during the 1930's the other eight were similarly rebuilt to LNER Class K2.

Superheating was installed at building though the boiler diameter at only 4ft 9₂ in. could only accommodate an 18-element Schmidt type. Two 20in. x 26in. outside cylinders with Walschaerts valve gear proved to be adequate for the engine and this size and combination of cylinders continued with the later H3 (K2) engines; Gresley was yet to introduce his 3-cylinder designs. No.1630 was in fact Gresley's first design for the GNR.

Driving wheels were 5ft 8in. in diameter, whilst the pony truck wheels were of 3ft 2in. diameter (No.1630 had 3ft 8in. wheels on the pony truck). Ideal for fast goods service, the driving wheel diameter was also useful for passenger excursion service and special traffic.

The original chimney height was reduced after Grouping to give an overall height from rail level of 12ft 10in., enabling them to work on the former GER territory of the LNER. However those that did migrate to the GE Section were soon displaced by similarly modified K2's.

Until 1927 all were fitted with piston tail rods inside a protective cover. However, when ex works 29th January 1927, No.4630's tail rods had been taken off and the other seven lost them whilst still K1 class.

All had the Class B 3500 gallons tender with unequal axle spacing in LNER days, mostly of the later type without handgrips, although there were many changes to and from those with handgrip. When new in February 1913, No.1633 seems to have been an exception in having an early Class B 3670 gallons tender coupled to it, and without handgrip.

Until during the 1914-18 war all had green paint and full lining. During that conflict they were painted grey without lining and with white letters and figures. By Grouping most if not all had regained green livery with lining. But from 1924 black livery with single red lining became the standard for their mixed traffic status though none were apparently ever noted with the lining.

Colwick got the bulk allocation of the first ten engines mainly for work on the fast goods trains to and from Manchester and Liverpool in which the GN had invested so much. King's Cross had three and Doncaster a solitary example. The London based engines worked passenger services of a local nature into Hertfordshire at least, between their braked goods workings but when the K2 was introduced in 1914 the three K1's were sent away in favour of four K2's. At Grouping, with two K1 rebuilt to K2, the allocation of the eight remaining K1 saw them dispersed to all points of the former GN system with Colwick still having three examples.

Between 1931 and 1937 the eight K1 were all rebuilt to K2 standard and Class K1 became extinct though as will be seen later it was revived again first by a solitary rebuild of another Gresley design and then later by a new class of LNER designed 2-cylinder 2-6-0 built in early BR days.

GRESLEY K2

In 1914 a larger boilered version of Gresley's H2 was introduced. Doncaster turned out ten of these engines, numbered 1640 to 1649 and designated H3 by the GNR (LNER K2), during that year. In 1916 another ten, 1650 to 1659 with Works numbers 1466 to 1475 were built at Doncaster. In 1918 another twenty H3 were supplied by the North British Locomotive Co., ten from their Hyde Park workshops, with many parts supplied by both Doncaster and Beyer, Peacock at Gorton (the original contractor), and ten built at the Queen's Park Works with supplied parts. In 1921 Kitson & Co. at Leeds built a further twenty-five engines which varied slightly from the other, earlier, engines in having Ross 'Pop' safety valves fitted in lieu of the Ramsbottom type which would be eventually replaced. All the contractor built engines had their tenders made at Doncaster.

The larger boiler diameter of the H3 enabled the bigger 24-element Robinson type superheater to be fitted, with a consequential increase in performance.

Starting in April 1921, seven engines were fitted for oil burning during the Miner's strike but all had the gear stripped out by November of the same year as coal supplies returned to normal. Though two different types of burner were in use the tender tanks all appeared the same.

Like the K1 class, the K2 engines had their overall height reduced to enable them to work over former GE lines but this lowering of chimney, dome, cab and whistle enabled the K2 to also take up employment on the ex-North British Railway lines of the LNER, particularly on the West Highland where a large proportion of them stayed until withdrawal.

It was because of their employment in Scotland that the biggest change in appearance took place when side window cabs were fitted to all the Scottish based engines. Whilst those used on the GE had the Westinghouse brake fitted.

From December 1933, those engines allocated to Eastfield shed were fitted with drop grates so that advantage could be taken of the wet ash pits at that depot. Eventually fifteen engines had been equipped over the sixteen year period up to December 1949 when No.61786 became the last K2 to receive such equipment.

Three of the class were officially recorded as being fitted with a speed indicator but no photograph supporting this has been found. No.1646 is said to have had a Flaman type put on in October 1919. In April 1934 it was recorded at Cowlairs that a Smith's type had been transferred from 4674 to 4700 and in October 1938 that it was still on 4700.

Because withdrawal of K2 class did not begin until September 1955 (61722), ten new boilers were built as late as April 1952 to May 1953. These boilers had BR numbers 21178 to 21187 but covers for the handholes were not provided.

One engine No.1630 was built at Doncaster August 1912 and is seen here as new. The Schmidy superheater had a damper, and twin anti-vacuum valves were fitted. At the side of the firebox the frame had two lightening holes but no extra access holes. The smokebox was 4ft 6¼in. long and the 1ft 11¼in. tall chimney gave a height from rail of 13ft 3⅞in. The pony truck had 3ft 8in. diameter wheels and the sanding to leading and driving wheels was steam applied. The tender was from the last batch of Class B to have side sheets curved down at the front and fitted with hand grip.

Ten engines numbered 1640 to 1649 were built at Doncaster between April and June 1914. The 5ft 6in. diameter boiler and 24 element Robinson superheater needed frames 5½in. longer than those on K1 class. Journals were 8¼in. diameter by 9in. long.

From 1947 many K2 tenders were fitted by Cowlairs with an additional vertical handrail at the left hand rear corner. This extra rail was only fitted to the nearside and none got it on the offside.

Up to Grouping the class was employed mainly on GN main line fast goods trains and mixed traffic duties with Doncaster and New England having the bulk of the various batches as they came into traffic and in late 1922 had twenty-odd K2's allocated to each shed. During the Miner's strike of 1921 these engines gained some glory when they were called upon to haul main line express passenger trains which in most cases were heavy 'combined' trains.

In 1924 six engines went to the GE Section as the newly arrived K3 class engines took over the No.1 goods turns. During 1924/25 another fourteen K2's went to the NB Section where they were to spend the rest of their working lives for the next thirty-odd years. These Scottish based engines were followed in 1931/32 by another six with the West Highland line being their main sphere of activity, at first on goods but later on passenger services too. Up to seven of the twenty Scottish K2's were allocated to St Margarets shed for duties on fast freights over the Waverley and ECML routes to Newcastle, with similar workings to Glasgow. They were also employed locally on goods and at weekends could be found on excursion trains to all sorts of destinations within Scotland. During BR days they went in small numbers to such sheds as Dunfermline, Thornton Jct, Kitybrewster and Ferryhill. Parkhead had at least five of them in the 1950s though during the LNER period one of the Fort William engines had gone there.

Those engines working on the former Great Eastern lines could be found on both passenger and express freight duties with Stratford shed having the bulk of the GE Section batch. Cambridge, Norwich and Colchester sheds used them at varying periods during LNER days.

Even the Midland & Great Northern Joint shed at South Lynn had there employment for five years from the end of 1947. On that section they were used on regular diagrams between Lynn and Yarmouth but by the end of 1952 all six of the K2's had left for the GN Section.

Colwick engines worked west as far west as Stafford on passenger, goods and milk trains whilst those based at New England worked both the main line and the 'Loop' traffic through Lincolnshire.

Those based in the West Riding at Ardsley and Copley Hill would often work over to Manchester and Liverpool besides the more usual duties in the Leeds area which took them to Doncaster and east to Grimsby. Bradford and Copley Hill engines were used on the King's Cross express passenger trains as far as Wakefield or Doncaster.

Annesley, Mexborough and Liverpool (Brunswick) sheds all had K2's at one time or another during the 1920's. Mexborough kept a couple in 1929 to be followed by others in the 1930's of which most stayed until 1940. At that shed they were employed mainly on local and intermediate distance passenger duties as far as Grimsby.

In 1942 those engines still working on the former GN lines of the LNER, numbering thirty-two, were concentrated at four sheds, Boston, Colwick, Doncaster and New England with Doncaster having no less than fifteen of them.

The first K2 to show LNER ownership was No.1645, ex works 27th January 1923. Although the first meeting of the Directors to choose standard livery did not take place until the 31st, and this K2 was not amongst the seven engines paraded for inspection. Therefore it is curious, and almost suspicious,

that 1645 was in exactly the style which became standard for passenger classes. Only one other K2 was painted green by Doncaster after Grouping; as a result of being involved in a collision No.1703 was in works from 16th October 1922 to 10th February 1923 on which date it emerged in L&NER style green similar to No.1645.

With their mixed traffic status, black with red lining became the livery for these engines but after 1941 the red lining was not applied for economy reasons. The letters NE also replaced LNER.

From 1933 thirteen of the Scottish based engines were named after Scottish Lochs and from August 1947 some of these engines gained green lined livery as did other Scottish based engines. Even two Southern Area engines got green livery as they went through repair at Cowlairs; altogether ten engines got the LNER green lined livery and seven more Scottish engines got similar green livery, but with BRITISH RAILWAYS on the tender, before the practice was stopped in July 1948.

The BR livery for the K2 became lined black with, at first, BRITISH RAILWAYS on the tender followed from mid-August 1949 by the BR emblem and then finally, from August 1957, the crest which was only applied to twenty-five engines: 61738, 61740, 61741, 61742, 61745, 61747, 61755, 61756, 61761, 61763, 61764, 61766, 61769, 61772, 61773, 61779, 61782, 61784, 61786, 61787, 61788, 61789, 61790, 61792, 61794. The crest on the right hand side had the lion facing the wrong way and none of the K2's had this corrected before withdrawal.

Withdrawal was started in 1955 with the demise of 61722 but it was to be eight years before the K2 class was finally extinct when the last one, No.61756, was withdrawn in June 1962 some fifty years after the original GNR built 2-6-0 had entered traffic.

Note: The cutting-up venues of certain engines is somewhat obscure. Those which are confirmed are as set out in the tables but those which are not confirmed have a question mark alongside and, those engines for which no location is known have been left blank. If any reader can confirm or deny the data, the editor would be pleased to hear from them via the Publisher.

THOMPSON K1/1

This solitary engine was a rebuild from one of the six Gresley 3-cylinder K4's introduced in 1937. Outline drawings for a 2-cylinder engine based on the K4 had been prepared in February 1945 under Thompson's orders and in December of that year No.3445 emerged from Doncaster in the guise of what might be termed the prototype for the forthcoming new Class K1. Besides its straighter running plate, the engine carried a shortened version of the B1 class boiler which was pressed to 225 lb.

Modifications during its lifetime were few, the only noticeable thing being changes to the smokebox door which were usually coincidental with change of boiler. It kept its 3500 gallons tender from its previous existence and this was unchanged throughout its life except for some small modification to the rear division plate in the mid-1950's to stop coal spillage into the water filler space.

Keeping its former K4 name MACCAILIN MÓR, No.3445 was classified K1 but this was later changed to K1/1 in December 1946 in readiness for the seventy production batch K1 engines which were ordered in July of the following year

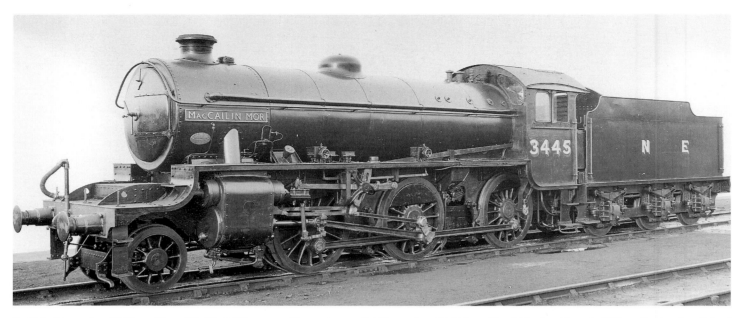

Built in December 1938 as Class K4, No.3445 was ex Doncaster on 1st December 1945 in unlined black with only NE on the tender. It had been rebuilt to Thompson ideas with two instead of three cylinders, shortened version of B1 class 225 lb. boiler and a pony truck with spring side control instead of Gresley swing link suspension. As Class K1 had been vacant since July 1937, No.3445 was given that classification, but from December 1946 it was altered to K1/1 to clear the way for the production batch to take Class K1. No.3445 was the only K4 rebuilt and it remained the single K1/1. Note the smokebox door was similar to that used by the first ten B1 class - 4ft 5¼in. diameter, 11ft radius curvature and with hinge straps 2ft apart on their centres.

In July 1947 the LNER ordered seventy Class K1 from North British Locomotive Co., Glasgow. Whilst they were only delivered from 30th May 1949 (62001) to 29th March 1950 (62070), they were all to LNER design and specification, based on the prototype K1/1 No.3445.

from the North British Locomotive Co. The reclassification coincided with renumbering, at Norwich shed, to 1997. It became 61997 at a light repair at Doncaster in January 1949.

Between 2nd December 1945 and 13th November 1949, it was allocated to various sheds in England and Scotland before settling down at Eastfield for work on the West Highland line. Before its permanent move to Scotland it was at Blaydon for a time and then twice at New England; these being amongst the sheds where the later Class K1 engines would be in greater numbers. In May 1954 it had a final move to Fort William.

All its heavy repairs were carried out at Doncaster whilst light repairs after 1949 were done at Cowlairs.

Coming out in wartime black with only NE on its tender, No.3445 got LNER and then during the BR period carried BRITISH RAILWAYS, the emblem and finally the crest - all on lined black.

Withdrawal took place in June 1961 at Doncaster after arriving in April for a heavy repair; it was cut-up at the 'Plant'.

PEPPERCORN K1

One of the youngest classes so far reviewed in this series, the Peppercorn K1 was an updated version of the Thompson rebuild Class K1/1. Most lasted out until the end of steam on the former LNER lines of British Railways and one was happily restored for preservation.

All seventy engines of the K1 class were built in Glasgow at the North British Locomotive Company's Queen's Park Works, being delivered in a ten month period between May 1949 and March 1950. As was the custom with NB built engines, they were at first sent the short distance to Eastfield shed for running-in before being sent south to England where they were set to work - thirty to the Eastern Region and forty to the North Eastern Region. Whilst at Eastfield they were used on all sorts of workings from short trip to express passenger turns.

The most noticeable difference from the 'prototype' engine (No.3445), was the cut away running plate in front of the cylinders, and the provision of a 4200 gallons tender which was found to be necessary after 1946 trials with 3445.

Electric lighting, with power supplied by a Stone's steam turbine, was standard on all engines from new and most kept this until withdrawal. Another standard fitting from new was a B.T.H. speed indicator but this did not fair too well and all had been taken off the class by the late 1950's.

A self-cleaning smokebox (SC plate placed below shed plate) was another innovation fitted to this class but steaming problems early on made modifications necessary though even this did not cure the problems completely, however, the apparatus was kept until withdrawal. Some, though not all, were fitted with AWS.

The first fifty engines came out in black with BRITISH RAILWAYS on the tender whilst the last twenty came out with the BR emblem. As they went into works for repair and repainting those without the emblem eventually got it. From 1957 the BR crest, including the incorrect and corrected version was carried by all the class.

Initial allocations saw ten engines going to Gorton shed but after a period of ten months these moved on to March joining the other twenty K1's allocated to the former GE Section where they settled down to both goods and passenger workings from that shed. They proved to be most satisfactory engines and were put to work on virtually all classes of traffic. Five of the March engines went to the West Highland line in February 1952 whilst the rest continued to work in England mainly from March in

the Eastern Region and Blaydon, Darlington, Heaton and Stockton sheds in the NE Region. Stratford shed thought so highly of the March K1's that they would regularly keep hold of the engines on summer weekends by various devious methods so that they could use them on excursion workings. In 1958 six of the March engines were finally allocated to Stratford but their stay in London was brief as diesel power was gradually taking over much of the steam workings from Stratford and indeed most of those in East Anglia and in the early 1960's, the March and Stratford engines began to move on to other sheds such as Frodingham, Retford and Doncaster where they were also welcomed and used on all types of traffic.

Doncaster maintained the K1's until November 1963 when Darlington took over. When Darlington closed Cowlairs continued to repair the engines and the last one to receive a repair, No.62059, was also the last steam locomotive repaired by Cowlairs. They gave it a coat of fresh paint before releasing it to traffic in September 1966.

Withdrawals had begun in December 1962 but it was to be another five years before the last engine, 62005 which was also the last Eastern Region steam engine, was withdrawn making Class K1 extinct once again. Happily 62005 was preserved though not in its BR guise. Instead it received LNER green livery and was numbered 2005.

Note: With reference to boiler renumbering. Where known these are listed in the tables as usual but because of lack of official data regarding the bulk of these renumberings, they have been left out purposely.

Features on the right hand side of No.1630 were the exposed reversing rod, and a mechanical lubricator for the cylinders and valves. However, until 1915 the axlebox journals had siphon oilboxes. Note the four washout plugs on each side of the firebox and that they were directly opposite each other.

No.1630 as at Grouping except that from 21st April 1923 it was fitted with a 1ft 5⅜in. tall chimney, bringing height from rail to 12ft 10in. so as to pass G.E. gauge, the highest point then being the dome at 13ft.

GRESLEY K1 CLASS (Rebuilt to K2)

4630

Doncaster 1354.

To traffic 8/1912.

REPAIRS:
Don. 6/7—11/11/22.**G.**
Don. 16—21/4/23.**L.**
New chimney to G.E. gauge.
Don. 5/12/23—15/3/24.**G.**
Don. 25/10/26—29/1/27.**G.**
Don. 19/10—16/11/29.**G.**
Don. 27/8—15/10/32.**G.**
Rebuilt to K2.
Don. 4/7—8/9/34.**G.**
Don. 25/4—16/5/36.**G.**
Don. 22/1—5/2/38.**G.**
Don. 23/12/39—27/1/40.**G.**
Don. 2—30/1/43.**G.**
Cow. 2/4—7/5/45.**G.**
Cow. 7/5—3/9/47.**G.**
Cow. 14/3—26/4/50.**G.**
Cow. ?/?—?/3/51.**C/L.**
Cow. 24/12/51—1/2/52.**G.**
Cow. 2/4—14/5/54.**G.**
Cow. 9—15/5/54.**C/L.**
Cow. 8/9—29/10/55.**C/L.**

BOILERS:
7172.
7190 (*ex1637*) 11/11/22.
7172 (*ex4633*) 29/1/27.
7250 (*exQ3 3420*) 15/10/32.
9075 (*new*) 5/2/38.
8865 (*ex4677*) 7/5/45.
9009 (*ex1753*) 3/9/47.
9009 reno. 21143 3/51.
21119 (*ex61746*) 1/2/52.
21150 (*ex61771*) 14/5/54.

SHEDS:
Colwick.
March *at* 5/24.
Colwick 30/7/25.
Cambridge 11/6/27.
New England 30/9/27
Grantham 30/12/30.
New England 9/11/32.
Boston 7/3/36.
New England 16/5/38.
Boston 17/6/43.
Colwick 16/4/45.
Immingham 27/4/47.
Boston 10/7/55.

RENUMBERED:
4630 15/3/24.
1720 12/5/46.
61720 26/4/50.

CONDEMNED: 12/6/56.
Cut up at Kilmarnock 5/57.

4631

Doncaster 1372.

To traffic 2/1913.

REPAIRS:
Don. 12/10/20—19/3/21.**G.**
Rebuilt to K2.
Don. 19/2—20/9/24.**G.**
New chimney to G.E. gauge.
Don. 31/3—1/10/26.**G.**
Str. ?/?—?/12/27.**L.**
Westinghouse brake fitted.
Don. 23/2—13/4/29.**G.**
Don. 14/5—25/6/32.**G.**
Don. 9/3—6/4/35.**G.**
Don. 15/5—19/6/37.**G.**
Don. 30/12/39—10/2/40.**G.**
Don. 7/11—12/12/42.**G.**
Don. 5—12/6/43.**L.**
Don. 5/2—4/3/44.**G.**
Cow. 1/5—15/6/46.**H.**
Cow. 5/1—20/2/47.**G.**
Cow. 23/6—4/9/48.**G.**
Cow. 1/3—7/4/51.**H/I.**
Cow. 17—19/4/51.**N/C.**
Cow. 17/10—23/11/51.**N/C.**
Cow. 16/12/53—22/1/54.**G.**
Westinghouse brake removed.
Cow. 28/12/55—28/1/56.**H/I.**
WPU gear removed
Cow. 6/2—17/3/56.**C/L.**
Dfu. 26/6—11/7/57.**C/L.**

BOILERS:
7184.
7550 (*new*) 19/3/21.
7837 (*new*) 1/10/26.
7840 (*ex4664*) 25/6/32.
8826 (*new*) 6/4/35.
9150 (*ex4683*) 4/3/44.
9476 (*new*) 15/6/46.
9476 reno. 21177 7/4/51.
21112 (*ex61737*) 22/1/54.

SHEDS:
Colwick.

Cambridge *at* 5/24.
New England 30/9/27.
Stratford ?/?
Southend ?/?
Stratford 25/1/30.
Colchester 15/9/32.
Parkeston 3/4/34.
Colchester 14/11/35.
Norwich 5/2/36.
March 19/2/45.
Norwich 22/6/47.
Stratford 13/10/47.
Eastfield 3/6/51.
Dunfermline 20/1/52.

RENUMBERED:
4631 20/9/24.
1721 3/2/46.
61721 4/9/48.

CONDEMNED: 30/12/59.
*Sold for scrap to J.N.Connell,
Coatbridge, 3/60.*

4632

Doncaster 1373.

To traffic 2/1913.

REPAIRS:
Don. 5/4—12/5/23.**H.**
New chimney to G.E. gauge.
Don. 12/10—31/12/25.**G.**
Don. 20/12/27—24/2/28.**G.**
Don. 15/3—12/4/30.**G.**
Don. 27/8—8/10/32.**G.**
Don. 9/1—16/2/35.**G.**
Don. 3—31/10/36.**G.**
Rebuilt to K2.
Don. 15/10—5/11/38.**G.**
Don. 17/8—28/9/40.**G.**
Don. 7—28/3/42.**L.**
Don. 13/3—10/4/43.**G.**
Cow. 5/7—9/8/45.**H.**
Cow. 11/8/45—26/1/46.**L.**
Cow. 21/9—17/12/47.**G.**
Cow. 20/2—23/4/49.**L/I.**
Cow. 2/3—7/7/51.**G.**
Cow. 1/4—2/5/53.**L/I.**
Cow. 7—18/12/53.**C/L.**
Cow. 13—20/8/54.**C/L.**
Cow. 31/1—19/3/55.**G.**

BOILERS:
7183.

7188 (*ex1636*) 12/5/23.
7183 (*ex1634*) 31/12/25.
7188 (*ex spare*) 24/2/28.
8980 (*new*) 31/10/36.
8982 (*ex4670*) 28/9/40.
8760 (*ex4633*) 9/8/45.
8867 (*ex4659*) 17/12/47.
21137 (*ex61769*) 7/7/51.
21100 (*ex61726*) 19/3/55.

SHEDS:
King's Cross.
Doncaster 25/3/23.
Stratford *at* 5/24.
Colwick 17/4/26.
Doncaster 13/8/30.
Mexborough 9/10/30.
Doncaster 28/2/40.
Colwick 21/8/46.
Immingham 27/4/47.
Eastfield 11/3/51.
Parkhead 24/2/52.

RENUMBERED:
4632 31/12/25.
1722 26/1/46.
61722 23/4/49.

CONDEMNED: 22/9/55.
Into Cow. for cut up 9/55.

4633

Doncaster 1374.

To traffic 2/1913.

REPAIRS:
Don. 8/5—17/6/22.**L.**
Don. 14/8—13/10/23.**G.**
As 1633N.
Don. 2/6—12/7/24.**H.**
New chimney to G.E. gauge.
Don. 9/12/25—22/4/26.**G.**
Don. 18/8—6/10/28.**G.**
Don. 13/12/30—17/1/31.**G.**
Don. 26/11/32—21/1/33.**G.**
Rebuilt to K2.
Don. 11/5—8/6/35.**G.**
Don. 27/3—24/4/37.**G.**
Don. 10/12/38—14/1/39.**G.**
Don. 2—30/11/40.**G.**
Don. 24/5—21/6/41.**L.**
Don. 25/7—19/9/42.**G.**
Cow. 1/10—11/11/44.**G.**
Cow. 26/6—21/7/45.**L.**

Nine more, Nos.1631 to 1639 were built at Doncaster from February to April 1913 but by Grouping Nos.1631 and 1635 had been rebuilt to Class K2. They had 3ft 2in. pony truck wheels, the smokebox was 5ft 6in. long, two access holes were provided at the side of the firebox and sanding to leading wheels was now by gravity. On Nos.1631, 1632 and 1633 the eccentric rods were plain as on No.1630 but on Nos.1634 to 1639 they were fluted. Apart from No.1633 their tenders were Class B from the first ten to have side sheets without hand grip.

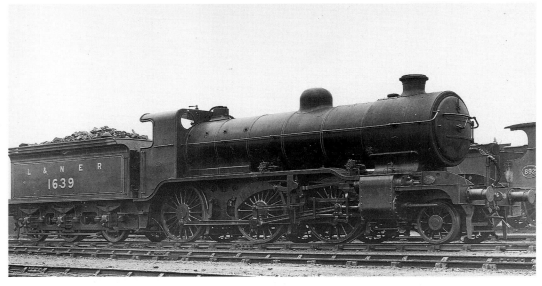

From 1915 the siphon oilboxes were replaced by a Wakefield mechanical lubricator to serve the axlebox journals. All eight were cut down to suit the former Great Eastern gauge: 1630 (21/4/23), 1632 (12/5/23), 1633N (13/10/23), 1634 (30/6/23), 1636 (14/4/23), 1637 (21/4/23), 4638 (16/8/24), 1639 (14/4/23).

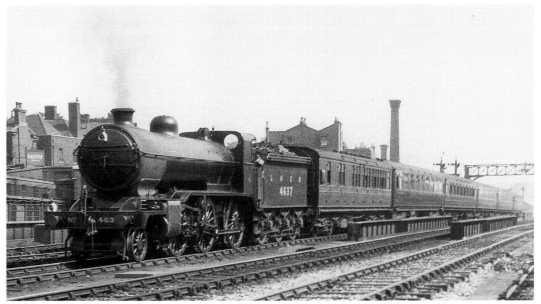

Although dust shields were standard on K2 class only Nos.4634 and 4637 were fitted with them whilst still K1 class. No.4637 got them in May 1927 and 4634 in August 1928.

Nos.1634 to 1639 had eccentric rods of fluted section and on Nos.1631 to 1639 the reversing rod was boxed instead of being exposed as on 1630.

The ten K1 boilers were not interchangeable with any other class, but the rebuilding of Nos.1631 and 1635 before Grouping provided two spares for exchange within the class. Between January 1927 and October 1928 the eight engines changed from Schmidt to Robinson header and inspection covers were put on the smokebox. At least five of the boilers were changed to three washout plugs on each side and on staggered pitching.

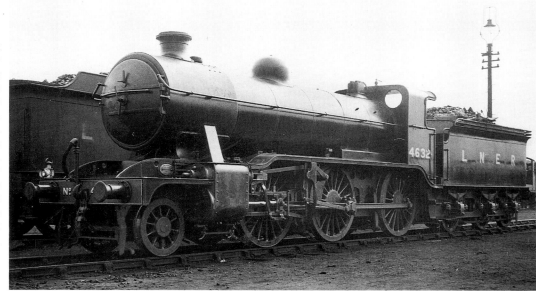

No.4630 which alone had shorter smokebox, kept that difference until the larger boiler was put on in October 1932. Ex works 29th January 1927, No.4630's tail rods had been removed. The other seven lost them whilst still K1 class.

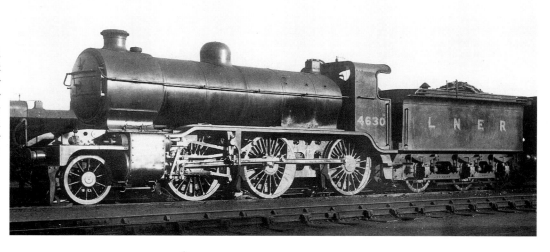

Cow. 1/11—8/12/45.**L.**
Cow. 28/11/46—11/4/47.**G.**
Cow. 10/1—26/3/49.**G.**
Cow. 28/3—23/6/51.**G.**
Cow. 6/6—17/7/52.**C/H.**
Cow. 28/9—28/11/53.**G.**
Cow. 4/10—3/12/55.**L/I.**
Cow. 8—25/6/56.**N/C.**

BOILERS:
7185.
7172 *(ex1630)* 13/10/23.
7191 *(ex1639)* 22/4/26.
7186 *(ex4634)* 6/10/28.
7184 *(ex4637)* 17/1/31.
7463 *(ex4686)* 21/1/33.
8760 *(ex4668)* 30/11/40.
9196 *(ex4640)* 11/11/44.
9201 *(ex1744)* 11/4/47.
21133 *(ex61722)* 23/6/51.
21149 *(ex61733)* 28/11/53.

SHEDS:
Colwick.
Stratford *at* 5/24.
Colwick 1/7/25.
Mexborough 14/1/31.
Doncaster 18/1/33.
Mexborough 6/3/33.
Doncaster 11/12/35.
March 4/11/37.
Doncaster 16/2/38.
Frodingham 4/7/43.
Doncaster 25/7/43.
Bradford 30/7/45.
Ardsley 30/12/45.
Bradford 30/6/46.
Colwick 18/8/46.

RENUMBERED:
4633 12/7/24.
1723 22/9/46.
61723 26/3/49.

CONDEMNED: 4/11/59.
Sold for scrap to Motherwell Machinery & Scrap, Wishaw, 2/60.

4634

Doncaster 1375.

To traffic 2/1913.

REPAIRS:
Don. 30/10/21—4/3/22.**L.**
Don. 11/5—30/6/23.**G.**
New chimney to G.E. gauge.
Don. 14/2—5/7/24.**G.**
Don. 22/3—19/7/26.**G.**
Don. 17/6—25/8/28.**G.**
Don. 28/3—20/6/31.**G.**
Rebuilt to K2.
Gor. 4—25/7/31.**L.**

Don. 2/12/33—6/1/34.**G.**
Don. 21/3—25/4/36.**G.**
Don. 26/2—12/3/38.**G.**
Don. 2/9—14/10/39.**G.**
Don. 23/11—21/12/40.**G.**
Don. 12/12/42—9/1/43.**G.**
Cow. 22/11—30/12/44.**G.**
Cow. ?/?—10/1/45.**L.**
Cow. 5/8—8/9/45.**L.**
Cow. 20/9—20/10/45.**L.**
Don. 26/10—30/11/46.**G.**
Cow. 1/1—11/2/50.**G.**
Cow. 18/6—8/7/52.**L/I.**
Cow. 1/10—5/11/52.**C/L.**
Cow. 4/3—17/4/54.**G.**
Cow. 4—12/5/54.**N/C.**
Cow. 20—22/5/54.**N/C.**
Cow. 16/11/57. *Not repaired.*

BOILERS:
7186.
7183 *(ex1632)* 30/6/23.
7186 *(ex spare)* 5/7/24.
7190 *(ex4630)* 25/8/28.
7548 *(ex4648)* 20/6/31.
8866 *(ex4673)* 12/3/38.
8978 *(ex4643)* 21/12/40.
9010 *(ex4680)* 9/1/43.
8558 *(ex61786)* 11/2/50.
8558 reno. 21108 8/7/52.
21133 *(ex61723)* 17/4/54.

SHEDS:
Ardsley.
Stratford *at* 5/24.
Colwick 22/6/25.
New England 23/8/27.
Doncaster 10/5/29.
Mexborough 16/5/29.
Doncaster 7/12/35.
Frodingham 4/7/43.
Doncaster 25/7/43.
Colwick 23/8/46.
Immingham 27/4/47.
Darnall 10/7/55.

RENUMBERED:
4634 5/7/24.
1724 26/7/46.
61724 11/2/50.

CONDEMNED: 3/1/58.
Cut up at Cowlairs ?

4635

Doncaster 1376.

To traffic 3/1913.

REPAIRS:
Don. ?/?—12/6/20.**G.**
Rebuilt to K2.
Don. 11/12/22—20/1/23.**L.**
Don. 1/10/24—31/1/25.**G.**

Don. 19/10/26—11/2/27.**G.**
Don. 22/6—3/8/29.**G.**
Don. 5/9—17/10/31.**G.**
Don. 20/5—24/6/33.**G.**
Don. 19/1—16/2/35.**G.**
Don. 7/11—5/12/36.**G.**
Don. 24/12/38—21/1/39.**G.**
Don. 2/3—6/4/40.**G.**
Don. 1—22/11/41.**L.**
Don. 28/3—2/5/42.**G.**
Cow. 1—30/9/44.**G.**
Cow. 19/7—18/8/45.**L.**
Cow. 5/2—23/3/46.**L.**
Cow. 1/6—27/11/47.**G.**
Cow. 26/4—17/6/50.**G.**
Cow. 2—8/7/50.**N/C.**
Cow. 22/5—21/6/52.**L/I.**
Cow. 22/8—5/9/52.**C/L.**
Cow. 25/2—30/4/55.**G.**

BOILERS:
7187.
7546 *(new)* 12/6/20.
7839 *(new)* 11/2/27.
7467 *(ex4640)* 17/10/31.
7452 *(ex4668)* 24/6/33.
7683 *(ex4645)* 21/1/39.
9198 *(new)* 6/4/40.
8979 *(ex4657)* 30/9/44.
9153 *(ex1728)* 27/11/47.
8843 *(ex1768)* 17/6/50.
8843 reno. 21122 21/6/52.
21143 *(ex61729)* 30/4/55.

SHEDS:
Colwick.
New England 29/7/25.
Boston 17/7/40.
New England 16/4/45.
Boston 4/8/46.

RENUMBERED:
4635 31/1/25.
1725 29/9/46.
61725 17/6/50.

CONDEMNED: 26/1/58.
Cut up at Kilmarnock ?

4636

Doncaster 1377.

To traffic 3/1913.

REPAIRS:
Don. 15/9—27/11/20.**G.**
Don. 1/2—14/4/23.**G.**
New chimney to G.E. gauge.
Don. 1/9/24—7/1/25.**G.**
Don. 12/2—1/5/26.**G.**
Don. 25/4—28/6/28.**G.**
Don. 31/5—19/7/30.**G.**
Don. 13/5—17/6/33.**G.**
Don. 20/7—31/8/35.**G.**

Don. 12/6—17/7/37.**G.**
Rebuilt to K2.
Don. 13/5—24/6/39.**G.**
Don. 31/5—5/7/41.**G.**
Don. 16/1—20/2/43.**G.**
Cow. 1—31/3/45.**G.**
Cow. 9/3—28/6/47.**G.**
Cow. 15/5—25/6/49.**G.**
Cow. 11/4—18/8/51.**G.**
Cow. 6—20/1/54.**H/I.**
Don. 18/6—28/7/54.**C/L.**
Cow. 21/11—25/12/54.**G.**
Cow. 27—31/12/54.**N/C.**
Don. 9/7—22/8/55.**C/L.**
Don. 17/2—10/3/56.**C/L.**

BOILERS:
7188.
7189 *(ex1638)* 14/4/23.
7183 *(ex4632)* 19/7/30.
9009 *(new)* 17/7/37.
8559 *(ex4646)* 31/3/45.
9344 *(ex1780)* 28/6/47.
21100 *(ex61783)* 18/8/51.
21106 *(ex61774)* 25/12/54.

SHEDS:
New England.
Stratford *by* 12/7/23.
Colwick 7/8/25.
Mexborough 29/7/30.
Doncaster 27/2/40.
Colwick 23/8/46.

RENUMBERED:
4636 7/1/25.
1726 6/10/46.
61726 25/6/49.

CONDEMNED: 7/5/57.

4637

Doncaster 1378.

To traffic 3/1913.

REPAIRS:
Don. ?/?—?/4/20.**G.**
Don. 6/7—18/11/22.**G.**
Don. 16—21/4/23.**L.**
New chimney to G.E. gauge.
Don. 29/10/24—14/2/25.**G.**
Don. 11/3—21/5/27.**G.**
Don. 6/4—11/5/29.**G.**
Don. 15/8—26/9/31.**G.**
Don. 21/4—19/5/34.**G.**
Don. 25/4—30/5/36.**G.**
Rebuilt to K2.
Don. 25/6—16/7/38.**G.**
Don. 8—29/6/40.**G.**
Don. 26/9—24/10/42.**G.**
Cow. 5/10—4/11/44.**G.**
Cow. 1/11—22/12/45.**G.**
Cow. 24/3—25/4/48.**G.**

The original boilers had Ramsbottom safety valves and in only one instance was any change made. Whilst still K1, three were changed to a later pattern of cylinder which had outside steam pipes. These were 4632 (8/10/32), 4638 (1/8/31) and 4639 (by 12/33).

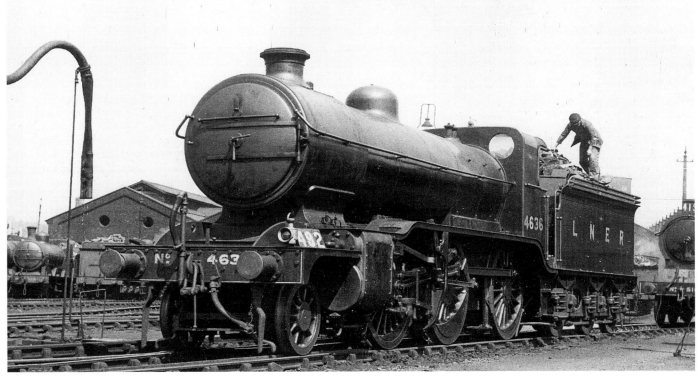

The safety valve change was on No.4636 from 19th July 1930 when Ross 'Pops' were put on a special raised seat because they could not be fitted directly to a boiler drilled to take Ramsbottom type. The boiler was one of those altered from four to three washout plugs.

For good measure No.4633's vacuum standpipe carried load class collars for both GNR and LNER systems. It had E1 from GN days and 3 for the LNER system introduced in August 1924 for Southern Area freight workings.

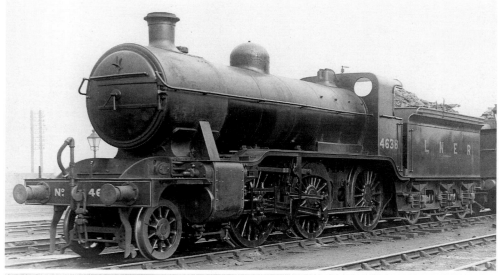

Although No.4638 had the 6in. shorter chimney fitted when ex works 16th August 1924, unlike the others, it was never transferred to a G.E. Section shed and when it was ex works 1st August 1931 the 1ft 11¼in. chimney was again on this engine, the only one to revert.

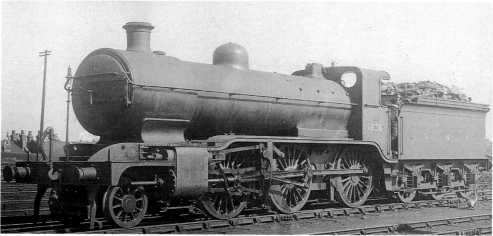

Until during the 1914-18 war all had green paint and full lining but at some time during the war they were painted grey without lining and with white letters and figures. However, by Grouping, most if not all had regained the green livery with lining.

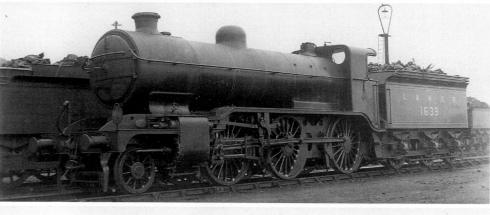

Ex works 17th February 1923, No.1639 was still green but with LNER style lining, the tender panel having rounded instead of scalloped corners. It was the last to be painted green and remained so to 3rd June 1925. Nos.1636 (14/4/23) and 1632 (12/5/23) got L&NER but on black, and 1634 had LNER (30/6/23). On 13th October 1923 No.1633ɴ was out but 4630 (15/3/24), 4637 (14/2/25) and 4638 (16/8/24) had the new numbering.

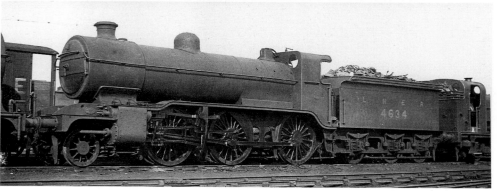

From February 1924 to March 1929 this was standard livery. As mixed traffic engines they were entitled to red lining but photographs show no evidence of this.

No.4634 became K2 from 20th June 1931 before the number was moved from tender to cab but the other seven carried the number on the cab side. On the tender 12in. figures were used but on the cab they were reduced to 9in. size. When No.4636 went to works on 12th June 1937 Class K1 became extinct.

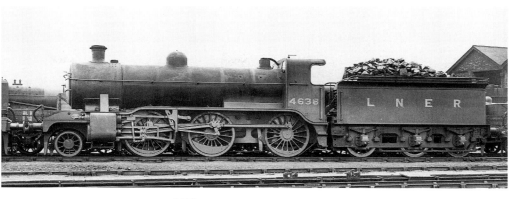

Cow. 1/8—25/9/49.**L/I**.
Cow. 14/7—17/9/51.**G**.
Cow. 17/10—18/11/53.**G**.
Cow. 21/2—13/3/54.**N/C**.

BOILERS:
7190.
7187 *(ex1635)* ?/4/20.
7184 *(ex1638)* 14/2/25.
7191 *(ex4633)* 11/5/29.
8869 *(new)* 30/5/36.
9350 *(new)* 24/10/42.
9193 *(ex4663)* 22/12/45.
8982 *(ex1749)* 25/4/48.
8982 reno. 21141 17/9/51.
21188 *(ex61742)* 18/11/53.

SHEDS:
New England.
Doncaster 25/3/23.
Colwick 22/7/25.
Doncaster 11/5/29.
Mexborough 16/5/29.
Doncaster 27/5/36.
Mexborough 21/7/36.
Doncaster 27/2/40.
Frodingham 4/7/43.
Doncaster 25/7/43.
Ardsley 30/7/45.
Colwick 18/8/46.
Immingham 27/4/47.

RENUMBERED:
4637 14/2/25.
1727 28/7/46.
61727 24/4/48.

CONDEMNED: 6/6/56.

4638

Doncaster 1379.

To traffic 4/1913.

REPAIRS:
Don. 16/6—8/10/21.**G**.
Don. 21/2—16/8/24.**G**.
New chimney to G.E. gauge.
Don. 8/11/26—10/2/27.**G**.
Don. 18/10—22/12/28.**G**.

Don. 13/6—1/8/31.**G**.
Don. 22/7—2/9/33.**G**.
Don. 28/12/35—8/2/36.**G**.
Rebuilt to K2.
Don. 13/2—6/3/37.**L**.
Don. 7—21/5/38.**G**.
Don. 13/7—17/8/40.**G**.
Don. 9/1—6/2/43.**G**.
Cow. 1/2—3/3/45.**G**.
Cow. 10/5—1/11/47.**G**.
Cow. 7/7—16/9/50.**G**.
Cow. 9/8—8/9/51.**C/L**.
Cow. 29/12/52—17/1/53.**H/I**.
Cow. 3/2—27/3/54.**G**.
Cow. 19/8—27/9/54.**C/L**.
Cow. 28/1—8/3/57.**H/I**.

BOILERS:
7189.
7184 *(ex1631)* 8/10/21.
7185 *(ex1633)* 16/8/24.
7184 *(ex4633)* 2/9/33.
8864 *(new)* 8/2/36.
7942 *(ex4656)* 6/2/43.
9153 *(ex4691)* 3/3/45.
9348 *(ex1751)* 1/11/47.
9153 *(ex1725)* 16/9/50.
9153 reno. 21153 17/1/53.
21130 *(ex61785)* 27/3/54.

SHEDS:
Colwick.
Doncaster 1/11/33.
Mexborough 27/4/35.
Doncaster 28/2/40.
Colwick 23/8/46.
Immingham 27/4/47.
Boston 15/3/53.
Darnall 10/7/55.

RENUMBERED:
4638 16/8/24.
1728 29/1/46.
61728 16/9/50.

CONDEMNED: 6/12/60.
Into Don. for cut up 6/12/60.

4639

Doncaster 1380.

To traffic 4/1913.

REPAIRS:
Don. 17/10/22—17/2/23.**G**.
Don. 3—14/4/23.**L**.
New chimney to G.E. gauge.
Don. 3/6—10/10/25.**G**.
Don. 21/10/27—14/1/28.**G**.
Don. 28/9—16/11/29.**G**.
Don. 6/6—11/7/31.**G**.
Don. 4/11—16/12/33.**G**.
Don. 9/11—7/12/35.**G**.
Rebuilt to K2.
Don. 13/11—4/12/37.**G**.
Don. 2—30/3/40.**G**.
Don. 31/10—12/12/42.**G**.
Cow. 8/3—29/4/44.**L**.
Cow. 12/3—14/4/45.**H**.
Cow. 16/1/46.**N/C**.
Cow. 15/1—22/2/47.**G**.
Cow. 28/6/47.**N/C**.
Spark arrestor fitted.
Cow. 20/11—5/12/47.**C/L**.
Cow. 21/3—23/4/48.**L/I**.
Cow. 5—6/10/48.**L**.
Cow. 21/7—1/10/49.**G**.
Alteration to cab side window.
Cow. 2/2—29/3/52.**G**.
Cow. 24/3—10/4/53.**C/L**.
Cow. 14/9—25/10/54.**G**.
Cow. 21/11—4/12/54.**N/C**.

BOILERS:
7191.
7187 *(ex1637)* 10/10/25.
8862 *(new)* 7/12/35.
8860 *(ex4650)* 4/12/37.
8869 *(ex4637)* 12/12/42.
8866 *(ex4680)* 14/4/45.
8977 *(ex1740)* 1/10/49.
21143 *(ex61720)* 29/3/52.
21108 *(ex61724)* 25/10/54.

SHEDS:
Colwick.
Stratford *by* 9/23.

Colwick 15/8/25.
New England 4/8/30.
Grantham 9/10/30.
New England 31/12/30.
Ardsley 14/7/31.
New England 17/8/31.
Grantham 14/6/32.
New England 27/12/35.
Boston 10/3/36.
New England 29/9/38.
Eastfield 14/12/45.
Parkhead 14/12/47.
New England 13/11/49.
Grantham 19/11/50.
Colwick 21/1/51.

RENUMBERED:
4639 10/10/25.
1729 28/4/46.
61729 1/10/49.

CONDEMNED: 25/6/57.

Ten more engines numbered 1650 to 1659 were completed at Doncaster between January and December 1916. The journals on these engines were increased to 9½in. diameter by 11in. long and Wakefield mechanical lubricators were fitted to serve them. As on the previous ten, the live steam pipes to the cylinders were out of sight between the frames.

Twenty engines numbered 1660 to 1679 were completed by North British Locomotive Co., Glasgow between June and August 1918. They were built with material supplied by Doncaster and by Beyer, Peacock with whom the order had been placed in June 1915. The order and material were transferred to N.B. Loco. in November 1917 for engines only as the GNR sent tenders to the makers. These twenty had outside steam pipes in a boxed shaped cover, and Detroit sight feed lubricators in the left hand side of the cab to serve them.

GRESLEY K2 CLASS

4640

Doncaster 1425.

To traffic 4/1914.

REPAIRS:
Don. 15/9/21—7/1/22.**G.**
Don. 1—27/1/23.**L.**
Don. 28/8—31/12/24.**G.**
Don. 30/4—30/5/25.**H.**
Don. 14/10/26—5/2/27.**G.**
Don. 11/12/28—9/2/29.**G.**
Don. 30/5—27/6/31.**G.**
Don. 18/3—29/4/33.**G.**
Don. 19/5—7/7/34.**G.**
Don. 22/2—21/3/36.**G.**
Don. 5/3—2/4/38.**G.**
Don. 27/1—24/2/40.**G.**
Don. 28/3—9/5/42.**G.**
Cow. 30/4—3/6/44.**G.**
Cow. 29/5—28/6/45.**L.**
Cow. 6/6—24/7/46.**G.**
Cow. 20/10—17/12/48.**G.**
Cow. 20/8—1/10/51.**L/I.**
Cow. 30/11/51—29/3/52.**C/L.**
Cow. 15/12/53—17/1/54.**G.**
Cow. 16/5—27/6/55.**H/I.**

BOILERS:
7251.
7467 *(ex1676)* 5/2/27.
7265 *(ex4666)* 27/6/31.
8562 *(new)* 7/7/34.
8561 *(ex4663)* 2/4/38.
9196 *(new)* 24/2/40.
9199 *(ex4643)* 3/6/44.
9195 *(ex4668)* 24/7/46.
9195 reno. 21158 1/10/51.
21146 *(ex61731)* 17/1/54.

SHEDS:
Ardsley.
New England *at* 5/24.
Colwick 22/8/27.
Cambridge 19/3/36.
Colwick 7/10/36.
March 3/6/37.
Norwich 22/5/47.
Lowestoft 27/8/47.
Stratford 13/10/47.
Colchester 1/2/48.
Stratford 16/5/48.
New England 26/3/50.
Norwich 15/10/50.
Immingham 11/3/51.

RENUMBERED:
4640 31/12/24.
1730 10/11/46.
61730 17/12/48.

CONDEMNED: 20/8/57.

4641

Doncaster 1426.

To traffic 4/1914.

REPAIRS:
Don. 14/10—5/11/21.**G.**
Don. 20/2—11/6/23.**G.**
Don. 7/2—25/4/25.**G.**
Don. 12/5—16/8/27.**G.**
Don. 28/12/29—25/1/30.**G.**
Don. 9/7—6/8/32.**G.**
Don. 23/6—11/8/34.**G.**
Don. 18/4—9/5/36.**G.**
Don. 8—29/1/38.**G.**
Don. 30/12/39—27/1/40.**G.**
Don. 23/11—21/12/40.**L.**
Don. 18/4—16/5/42.**G.**
Don. 5/7—11/8/44.**G.**
Cow. 23/11/45—2/2/46.**G.**
Don. 4/7—16/11/46.**G.**
Cow. 7—18/12/47.**L.**
Cow. 4—31/1/48.**G.**
Cow. 7/6—6/8/50.**H/I.**
Cow. 1/9—18/10/52.**G.**
Cow. 12/1—13/2/56.**G.**

BOILERS:
7253.
7459 *(ex4668)* 16/8/27.
7257 *(ex4657)* 25/1/30.
8868 *(new)* 9/5/36.
9074 *(new)* 29/1/38.
9194 *(ex4670)* 11/8/44.
8844 *(ex4642)* 2/2/46.
8760 *(ex1722)* 31/1/48.
21173 *(ex61754)* 18/10/52.
21117 *(ex61757)* 13/2/56.

SHEDS:
New England *at* 12/23.
Colwick 4/8/30.
Boston 2/7/46.

RENUMBERED:
4641 25/4/25.
1731 15/12/46.
61731 5/8/50.

CONDEMNED: 22/6/59.
Sold for scrap to Motherwell Machinery & Scrap, Wishaw, 30/11/59.

4642

Doncaster 1428.

To traffic 4/1914.

REPAIRS:
Don. 24/1—20/5/22.**G.**
Don. 22/7—18/10/24.**G.**
Don. 22/6—11/8/25.**H.**
Don. 19/10—5/12/25.**L.**
Don. 3/8—9/10/26.**L.**
Don. 9/2—30/4/27.**G.**
Don. 23/3—18/5/29.**G.**
Don. 20/7—19/8/29.**L.**
Don. 21/3—25/4/31.**G.**
Don. 29/4—10/6/33.**G.**
Don. 29/6—27/7/35.**G.**
Don. 1/5—5/6/37.**G.**
Don. 4/2—11/3/39.**G.**
Don. 14/12/40—18/1/41.**G.**
Don. 10/4—8/5/43.**G.**
Cow. 1/10—2/12/44.**G.**
Cow. 13/4—27/9/47.**G.**
Cow. 20/6—25/8/49.**G.**
Cow. 25/9—1/10/49.**C/H.**
Cow. 9—13/10/49.**N/C.**
Cow. 27/12/51—17/3/52.**G.**
Cow. 24—25/3/52.**N/C.**
Gor. 11/11—5/12/53.**C/L.**
Cow. 7/6—16/7/54.**L/I.**
Cow. 1/9—22/10/55.**C/L.**
Cow. 22/2/57. *Not repaired.*

BOILERS:
7256.
7259 *(ex1670)* 11/8/25.
7458 *(ex4667)* 18/5/29.
8844 *(new)* 27/7/35.
9076 *(ex4678)* 8/5/43.
7686 *(ex4669)* 2/12/44.
8865 *(ex1720)* 27/9/47.
9152 *(ex1742)* 25/8/49.
9152 reno.21152 17/3/52.

SHEDS:
Doncaster.
Ardsley 30/7/45.
Bradford 19/8/45.
Ardsley 2/12/45.
Colwick 18/8/46.
Annesley 4/1/48.

Colwick 22/2/48.

RENUMBERED:
4642 18/10/24.
1732 13/8/46.
61732 25/8/49.

CONDEMNED: 10/4/57.
Cut up at Kilmarnock 5/57.

4643

Doncaster 1429.

To traffic 4/1914.

REPAIRS:
VcA. 24/2—22/7/21.**G.**
Don. 11/7—8/11/24.**G.**
Don. 22/8—7/11/25.**G.**
Don. 3/1—21/3/28.**G.**
Don. 1/2—15/3/30.**G.**
Don. 1/10—5/11/32.**G.**
Don. 22/9—13/10/34.**G.**
Don. 25/7—22/8/36.**G.**
Don. 23/4—7/5/38.**G.**
Don. 23/3—13/4/40.**G.**
Don. 21/6—2/8/41.**G.**
Don. 27/6—1/8/42.**G.**
Cow. ?/?—27/5/44.**G.**
Cow. ?/?—3/3/45.**L.**
Cow. 24/4—8/6/46.**G.**
Cow. 4/7—9/9/48.**G.**
Cow. 12/4—28/5/49.**C/H.**
Cow. 23/1—16/2/51.**H/I.**
Cow. 23—28/2/51.**N/C.**
Cow. 9—10/7/52.**N/C.**
Cow. 15/9—4/10/52.**C/L.**
Cow. 15/6—4/7/53.**G.**
Cow. 17/5—25/6/55.**L/I.**
Cow. 24/5—2/6/56.**C/L.**
Cow. 26/11/56—12/1/57.**H/I.**
Cow. 28—29/1/57.**N/C.**
Cow. 30/1—1/2/57.**N/C.**

BOILERS:
7252.
7254 *(ex1646)* 8/11/24.
7607 *(ex1686)* 7/11/25.
7266 *(ex4664)* 21/3/28.
8978 *(new)* 22/8/36.
9199 *(new)* 13/4/40.
8868 *(ex4673)* 27/5/44.
9075 *(ex4630)* 8/6/46.
9075 reno. 21149 16/2/51.
21186 *(new)* 4/7/53.

WORKS CODES:- Cw - Cowlairs. Dar- Darlington. Dfu - Dunfermline shed. Don - Doncaster. Etfd - Eastfied shed. Ghd - Gateshead. Gor - Gorton. Inv - Inverurie.
ThJ - Thornton Junction shed. Str - Stratford. VcA - Vickers Armstrong.
REPAIR CODES:- **C/H** - Casual Heavy. **C/L** - Casual Light. **G** - General. **H** - Heavy. **H/I** - Heavy Intermediate. **L** - Light. **L/I** - Light Intermediate. **N/C** - Non-Classified.

SHEDS:
New England.
Colwick *by* 1/29.
Immingham 27/4/47.
Eastfield 14/1/51.
Parkhead 21/1/51.

RENUMBERED:
4643 13/10/24.
1733 8/6/46.
61733 9/9/48.

CONDEMNED: 17/10/57.
Cut up at Kilmarnock.

4644

Doncaster 1430.

To traffic 4/1914.

REPAIRS:
Don. 1/6—1/10/21.**G.**
Don. 21/2—5/7/24.**G.**
New chimney fitted.
Don. 22/1—10/4/26.**G.**
Don. 8/11—18/12/26.**L.**
Str. ?/?—?/2/28.**L.**
Westinghouse brake fitted.
Don. 14/11/28—4/1/29.**G.**
Don. 30/8—11/10/30.**G.**
Don. 30/7—17/9/32.**G.**
Don. 6/4—4/5/35.**G.**
Don. 21/5—11/6/38.**G.**
Don. 13/5—22/7/39.**L.**
Don. 5/4—3/5/41.**G.**
Don. 10/7—14/8/43.**G.**
Cow. 28/6—10/8/45.**G.**
Cow. 20/6—20/9/47.**H/I.**
Cow. ?/5—12/6/48.**L.**
Cow. 7/1—10/2/51.**H/I.**
Cow. ?/?—19/1/52.**C/L.**
Side window cab fitted.
Westinghouse brake removed.
Cow. 12/9—1/11/52.**G.**
Cow. 2/6—8/7/54.**L/I.**

BOILERS:
7255.
7268 *(ex1653)* 5/7/24.
7255 *(ex4669)* 4/1/29.
7603 *(ex4661)* 17/9/32.
8562 *(ex4640)* 11/6/38.
8825 *(ex4698)* 10/8/45.
8825 reno. 21118 10/2/51.
21155 *(ex61765)* 1/11/52.

SHEDS:
New England.
Cambridge 7/24.
Stratford 15/10/27.
King's Cross 3/1/29.
Norwich 9/10/30.
Yarmouth 17/10/30.
King's Cross 28/12/30.

March 2/2/32.
Norwich 18/10/35.
March 18/2/45.
Stratford 2/10/47.
Eastfield 3/6/51.
Dunfermline 10/2/52.
Thornton Jct 16/11/52.
Aberdeen 10/5/53.
Keith 7/7/54.

RENUMBERED:
4644 5/7/24.
1734 26/5/46.
61734 12/6/48.

CONDEMNED: 25/7/56.
Cut up at Cowlairs?.

4645

Doncaster 1431.

To traffic 5/1914.

REPAIRS:
Don. ?/?—?/4/20.**G.**
Don. 5/10/22—27/1/23.**G.**
Green L&NER.
Don. 4/9/24—3/1/25.**G.**
Don. 19/2—28/4/26.**L.**
Don. 29/4—6/8/27.**G.**
Don. 16/2—20/4/29.**G.**
Don. 30/8—18/10/30.**G.**
Don. 14/11—12/12/31.**G.**
Don. 13/2—12/3/32.**L.**
Don. 18/11—16/12/33.**G.**
Don. 18/7—15/8/36.**G.**
Don. 29/10—26/11/38.**G.**
Don. 15/3—19/4/41.**G.**
Don. 14/8—11/9/43.**G.**
Don. 17—24/6/44.**L.**
Cow. 22/11/45—5/1/46.**G.**
Don. 22/2—2/4/48.**G.**
Cow. 29/5—16/8/48.**L.**
Cow. 29/1—24/2/51.**H/I.**
Side window cab fitted.
Cow. 20/3—7/4/51.**N/C.**
Cow. 24/6/52.**N/C.**
Cow. 29/12/52—27/1/53.**G.**
Cow. 16/8—18/9/54.**L/I.**

BOILERS:
7257.
7547 *(new)* ?/4/20.
7685 *(ex4652)* 6/8/27.
7683 *(ex4671)* 16/12/33.
9151 *(new)* 26/11/38.
8841 *(ex4667)* 5/1/46.
8841 reno. 21121 24/2/51.
21164 *(ex61748)* 27/1/53.

SHEDS:
King's Cross.
New England 29/2/40.
Doncaster 4/4/42.

Colwick 21/8/46.
Immingham 27/4/47.
New England 1/5/49.
Eastfield 14/1/51.
Parkhead 21/1/51.

RENUMBERED:
4645 3/1/25.
1735 23/2/46.
61735 2/4/48.

CONDEMNED: 21/1/57.
Cut up at Kilmarnock.

4646

Doncaster 1432.

To traffic 5/1914.

REPAIRS:
VcA. 4/3—27/8/21.**G.**
Don. 12/10/23—12/1/24.**G.**
Don. 2/1—14/3/25.**H.**
Don. 15/1—3/4/26.**G.**
Don. 24/6—29/9/27.**G.**
Don. 4/5—8/6/29.**G.**
Altered to G.E. gauge.
Don. 21/2—28/3/31.**G.**
Don. 24/6—29/7/33.**G.**
Don. 27/7—31/8/35.**G.**
Don. 19/6—24/7/37.**G.**
Don. 18/2—8/4/39.**G.**
Don. 29/6—13/7/40.**L.**
Don. 8/2—1/3/41.**G.**
Don. 10/10—7/11/42.**G.**
Cow. 19/12/44—3/2/45.**G.**
Don. 17—20/10/45.**L.**
Cow. 14/12/45—5/1/46.**L.**
Cow. ?/?—23/8/46.**L.**
Cow. 16/9—2/11/46.**G.**
Cow. 1/12/48—8/2/49.**G.**
Cow. 9/7—29/10/49.**C/H.**
Don. 2—9/3/50.**C/L.**
Don. 28/11—1/12/50.**N/C.**
Cow. 14/11—24/12/51.**G.**
Cow. 17/2—15/3/53.**G.**
Cow. 17/5—24/6/55.**H/I.**

BOILERS:
7254.
7469 *(ex1678)* 12/1/24.
7451 *(ex4651)* 8/6/29.
7469 *(ex spare)* 28/3/31.
7840 *(ex4631)* 31/8/35.
8559 *(ex4660)* 8/4/39.
7622 *(ex4703)* 3/2/45.
9199 *(ex4640)* 2/11/46.
9073 *(ex1785)* 8/2/49.
9073 reno. 21146 24/12/51.
21121 *(ex61735)* 15/3/53.

SHEDS:
New England.
Colwick ?/?

King's Cross 20/6/25.
Colwick 8/6/29.
Cambridge 6/3/36.
Colwick 6/10/36.
Doncaster 29/2/40.
Boston 7/4/46.
New England 16/6/46.
Boston 7/1/51.
Immingham 20/5/51.

RENUMBERED:
4646 14/3/25.
1736 2/2/46.
61736 5/2/49.

CONDEMNED: 7/5/57.

4647

Doncaster 1433.

To traffic 5/1914.

REPAIRS:
Don. 25/8—17/12/21.**G.**
Don. 14/5—4/10/24.**G.**
New chimney to G.E. gauge.
Don. 15/6—22/10/26.**G.**
Str. 7—14/9/27.**N/C.**
Westinghouse brake fitted.
Don. 27/9—15/11/28.**G.**
Don. 5/7—23/8/30.**G.**
Don. 25/3—6/5/33.**G.**
Don. 13/4—25/5/35.**G.**
Don. 3—31/7/37.**G.**
Don. 16/4—7/5/38.**G.**
Don. 14/12/40—11/1/41.**G.**
Don. 8/5—5/6/43.**G.**
Cow. 8—29/4/45.**G.**
Str. 15/6—7/7/45.**L.**
Cow. 3/11—8/12/45.**L.**
Cow. 22/3—13/7/46.**L.**
Cow. 21/10—26/12/47.**H.**
Cow. 14/7—19/9/50.**H/I.**
Cow. 19/12/51—1/1/52.**C/L.**
Cow. 1/7—11/8/53.**G.**
Cow. 7/10—27/11/53.**C/L.**
Cow. 7/5—26/6/54.**C/L.**
Cow. 23/9—16/10/54.**C/L.**
Cow. 14/11/56. *Not repaired.*

BOILERS:
7258.
7683 *(new)* 4/10/24.
7453 *(ex4654)* 23/8/30.
7255 *(ex4644)* 6/5/33.
8560 *(ex4676)* 31/7/37.
8757 *(ex spare)* 29/4/45.
21187 *(new)* 11/8/53.

SHEDS:
New England.
Stratford *after* 4/10/24.
Southend 21/12/29.
Stratford 11/1/30.

(above) **Twenty-five engines numbered 1680 to 1704 were built by Kitson & Co., Leeds from June to September 1921, with the GN supplying the tenders for them. These engines differed from the previous batch by having Ross 'Pop' safety valves and no piston tail rods.**

(right) **Although equipped with Detroit sight feed lubricators like Nos.1660 to 1679, on Nos.1680 to 1704 the pipes from cab to cylinders were both along the left hand side of the boiler. On the right hand side there was only the mechanical lubricator for the axleboxes. The boilers on this batch of engines had the washout plugs 4in. further forward than on earlier boilers.**

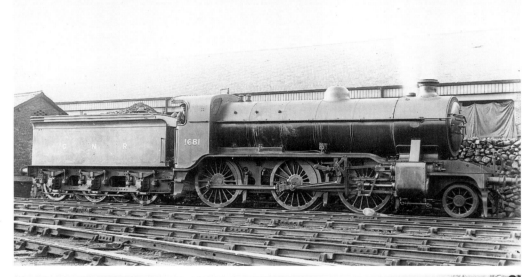

By Grouping the class had been increased by two re-boilered from K1, No.1635 ex works 12th June 1920 and 1631 ex works 19th March 1921. No alteration to frame length was made but a 24-element Robinson type superheater replaced the 18-element Schmidt type.

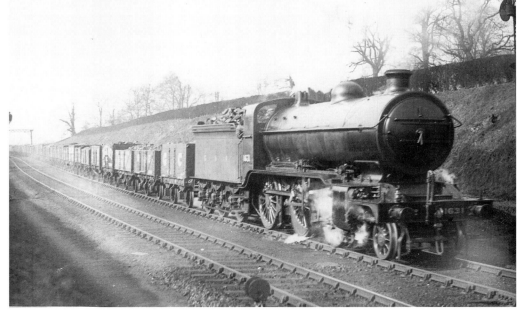

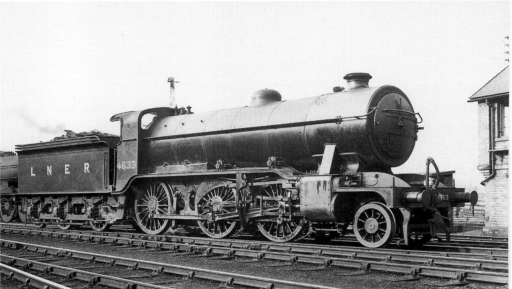

(above) **Reboilering from K1 class was resumed in 1931 and when No.4630 was out on 15th October 1932 it still had its unique 3ft 8in. diameter wheels on the pony truck, and retained inside steam pipes. The Class A tender was only a temporary coupling for repair.**

(left) **From June 1931 (No.4634) to July 1937 (No.4636) the other seven K1 were changed to K2. The larger diameter boiler needed the cab front windows altering from circular to shaped. Until 1934, boilers had three washout plugs at each side of the firebox. The three plugs on the right hand side were on staggered pitching to increase the area covered.**

Commencing with boiler No.8823, new on No.4659 when ex works 22nd December 1934, washout plugs were replaced by handholes, and on the right hand side only two were provided.

Yarmouth 2/10/31.
Stratford 22/12/31.
Norwich 12/12/41.
March 19/2/45.
Norwich 7/2/47.
Stratford 22/10/47.
New England 17/10/49.
Stratford 26/3/50.
Colwick 5/10/52.
Darnall 26/6/55.

RENUMBERED:
4647 4/10/24.
1737 13/4/46.
61737 9/9/50.

CONDEMNED: 22/11/56.
Cut up at Kilmarnock.

4648

Doncaster 1434.

To traffic 6/1914.

REPAIRS:
Don. ?/?—?/7/20.**G.**
Don. 30/11/22—4/5/23.**G.**
Don. 20/5—22/8/25.**G.**
Don. 24/9—1/12/27.**G.**
Don. 19/10—9/11/29.**G.**
Don. 11/7—8/8/31.**G.**
Don. 17/5—5/8/33.**G.**
Don. 29/6—3/8/35.**G.**
Don. 31/12/36—23/1/37.**G.**
Don. 18/12/38—1/4/39.**G.**
Don. 22/2—15/3/41.**G.**
Cow. 15/8—1/10/43.**G.**
Cow. 15/4—13/7/46.**G.**
Cow. 24/3—30/4/48.**G.**
Cow. 2—5/5/48.**N/C.**
Cow. 27/3—19/5/50.**G.**
Cow. 22/10—6/12/52.**H/I.**
Cow. 20/5—19/6/54.**C/L.**
Cow. 12/5—2/7/55.**G.**
Cow. 10/4—11/6/58.**H/I.**

BOILERS:
7259.
7548 *(new)* ?/7/20.
7268 *(ex4644)* 9/11/29.
8981 *(new)* 23/1/37.
7684 *(ex4698)* 1/10/43.
9347 *(ex4676)* 13/7/46.
9193 *(ex1727)* 30/4/48.
9010 *(ex1724)* 19/5/50.
9010 reno. 21144 6/12/52.
21142 *(ex61740)* 2/7/55.

SHEDS:
Ardsley.
New England ?/?
Ardsley ?/?
Doncaster 14/2/28.
March 19/5/37.

Norwich 7/2/47.
Lowestoft 26/3/47.
Stratford 13/10/47.
South Lynn 3/12/47.
Colwick 8/4/51.

RENUMBERED:
4648 22/8/25.
1738 24/3/46.
61738 8/5/48.

CONDEMNED: 3/7/59.
Into Dar. for cut up 9/59.

4649

Doncaster 1435.

To traffic 6/1914.

REPAIRS:
VcA. 24/2—15/8/21.**G.**
Don. 31/5—11/10/24.**G.**
Don. 23/8—6/12/26.**G.**
Don. 23/8—3/11/28.**G.**
Don. 12/4—24/5/30.**G.**
Don. 13/8—24/9/32.**G.**
Don. 8/10—4/11/33.**L.**
Don. 29/9—27/10/34.**G.**
Don. 16/1—13/2/37.**G.**
Don. 25/6—16/7/38.**G.**
Don. 27/4—18/5/40.**L.**
Don. 13/7—10/8/40.**G.**
Don. 22/11—20/12/41.**L.**
Don. 10/7—14/8/43.**G.**
Cow. 5/12/45—19/1/46.**G.**
Don. 21/9—5/10/46.**L.**
Cow. 9/10—6/12/47.**G.**
Cow. ?/?—?/1/48.**C/L.**
Cow. 4/10—22/11/50.**H/I.**
Cow. 20/7—11/9/52.**G.**
Cow. 16/12/52—21/1/53.**C/L.**
Cow. 14/8—26/9/53.**C/L.**
Cow. 6/12/54—15/1/55.**G.**
Cow. 17/3—4/5/55.**C/L.**
Dar. 20/2/59. *Not repaired.*

BOILERS:
7260.
7684 *(new)* 11/10/24.
7460 *(ex4677)* 24/5/30.
7686 *(ex4679)* 27/10/34.
8862 *(ex4663)* 10/8/40.
9011 *(ex4664)* 14/8/43.
9345 *(ex1745)* 6/12/47.
21180 *(new)* 11/9/52.
21163 *(ex61747)* 15/1/55.

SHEDS:
King's Cross.
New England 29/2/40.
Boston 6/10/41.
Colwick 16/4/45.
Immingham 27/4/47.
New England 1/5/49.

Boston 7/1/51.
Immingham 20/5/51.
Thornton Jct 25/1/53.
Immingham 25/3/53.
Darnall 10/7/55.
Colwick 2/6/57.

RENUMBERED:
4649 11/10/24.
1739 3/10/46.
61739 22/11/50.

CONDEMNED: 27/2/59.
Cut up at Darlington.

4650

Doncaster 1466.

To traffic 1/1916.

REPAIRS:
VcA. 4/3—21/9/21.**G.**
Don. 23/5—22/9/23.**G.**
As 1650N.
Don. 21/7—24/10/25.**G.**
Don. 22/10/27—6/1/28.**G.**
Don. 15/2—1/3/28.**L.**
Altered to G.E. gauge.
Westinghouse brake fitted.
Don. 8/3—12/4/30.**G.**
Don. 4/6—16/7/32.**G.**
Don. 12/10—16/11/35.**G.**
Don. 6—27/11/37.**G.**
Don. 28/10—2/12/39.**G.**
Don. 15/11—20/12/41.**G.**
Cow. 2/1—16/2/44.**G.**
Don. 18/11—2/12/44.**L.**
Cow. 25/10—14/12/45.**G.**
Str. 9/9/46—27/3/47.**L.**
Cow. 28/10/48—14/1/49.**G.**
Cow. 10/6—13/7/51.**H/I.**
Cow. 19/7—4/8/51.**C/L.**
Cow. 15/1—7/2/53.**L/I.**
Cow. 2/2—26/3/55.**G.**
Cow. 4/12/57—11/1/58.**H/I.**
Don. 1/1/61. *Not repaired.*

BOILERS:
7261.
7461 *(ex1670)* 22/9/23.
7606 *(ex4685)* 6/1/28.
7457 *(ex4658)* 12/4/30.
8860 *(new)* 16/11/35.
7838 *(ex4672)* 27/11/37.
8977 *(ex4701)* 16/2/44.
9008 *(ex4655)* 14/1/49.
9008 reno. 21142 13/7/51.
21151 *(ex61760)* 26/3/55.

SHEDS:
Doncaster.
Ardsley ?/?
Colwick 6/12/25.
King's Cross 25/4/26.

Stratford 7/3/28.
Yarmouth 26/9/30
Stratford 28/12/30.
Lowestoft 2/10/31.
Stratford 18/12/31.
March 9/5/38.
Norwich 22/6/47.
Stratford 17/10/47.
New England 18/10/49.
Immingham 7/1/51.
Colwick 12/6/60.

RENUMBERED:
4650 24/10/25.
1740 24/3/46.
61740 14/1/49.

CONDEMNED: 3/1/61.
Into Don. for cut up 3/1/61.

4651

Doncaster 1467.

To traffic 2/1916.

REPAIRS:
Don. 2/8—18/11/22.**G.**
Don. 15/12/24—28/3/25.**G.**
Don. 28/4—15/7/27.**G.**
Don. 13/4—18/5/29.**G.**
Don. 21/6—26/7/30.**G.**
Don. 5/11—3/12/32.**G.**
Don. 25/8—29/9/34.**G.**
Don. 20/6—18/7/36.**G.**
Don. 9—30/4/38.**G.**
Don. 1/7—5/8/39.**G.**
Don. 31/5—5/7/41.**G.**
Cow. ?/?—18/11/43.**G.**
Cow. ?/?—16/3/44.**L.**
Cow. ?/?—9/9/44.**L.**
Cow. ?/?—28/10/44.**L.**
Cow. 25/2—29/3/47.**G.**
Cow. ?/?—11/9/48.**L.**
Cow. 14/9—16/11/49.**H/I.**
Cow. 9/11—30/12/50.**G.**
Cow. 4—27/1/51.**C/L.**
Cow. 4—13/12/52.**N/C.**
Cow. 8—27/6/53.**L/I.**
Cow. 12/1/54.**N/C.**
ThJ. 10/6—3/7/54.**C/L.**
Cow. 9/11—10/12/55.**G.**
WPU gear removed.
Cow. 28/10—23/11/57.**H/I.**
Cow. 14—17/12/59.**N/C.**

BOILERS:
7263.
7451 *(ex1660)* 28/3/25.
7263 *(ex4674)* 18/5/29.
8758 *(new)* 29/9/34.
8863 *(ex4652)* 30/4/38.
8561 *(ex4640)* 5/7/41.
8981 *(ex4648)* 18/11/43.
9349 *(ex1750)* 29/3/47.

9348 *(ex1728)* 30/12/50.
9348 reno. 21170 27/6/53.
21147 *(ex61773)* 10/12/55.

SHEDS:
King's Cross.
Doncaster 3/11/25.
Colwick 12/8/30.
Boston 28/7/36
Colwick 1/9/36.
Doncaster 29/2/40.
Ardsley 30/7/45.
Colwick 18/8/46
Eastfield 28/1/51.
Thornton Jct 23/12/51.
Kittybrewster 5/3/57.

RENUMBERED:
4651 28/3/25.
1741 31/3/46.
61741 11/9/48.

CONDEMNED: 11/3/60.
Into Cow. for cut up 30/4/60.

4652

Doncaster 1469.

To traffic 5/1916.

REPAIRS:
VcA. 4/3—15/8/21.**G.**
Don. 11/3—9/8/24.**G.**
Altered to G.E. gauge.
Don. 13/4—23/7/27.**G.**
Westinghouse brake fitted.
Don. 16/2—27/4/29.**G.**
Str. 1/10—17/12/30.**L.**
Don. 19/3—30/4/32.**G.**
Don. 20/5—8/7/33.**G.**
Don. 3/2—24/3/34.**L.**
Don. 7/12/35—11/1/36.**G.**
Str. 26/3—6/4/36.**L.**
Don. 26/2—2/4/38.**G.**
Don. 4—18/6/38.**L.**
Don. 22/2—22/3/41.**G.**
Don. 29/3—4/4/41.**N/C.**
Don. 20/3—10/4/43.**G.**
Don. 12/6—17/7/43.**L.**
Str. 19/6—27/7/44.**L.**
Cow. 9/9—20/10/45.**G.**
Cow. 19/2—22/5/47.**G.**
Cow. 26/10—8/11/47.**L.**
Cow. 31/5—2/9/49.**G.**
Cow. 27/1—25/2/50.**C/H.**
Cow. 5—9/3/50.**N/C.**
Cow. 5/7—23/8/51.**L/I.**
Cow. 27/3—9/5/53.**G.**
Cow. 24/5—24/7/55.**H/I.**
Cow. 3—4/8/55.**N/C.**
Cow. 20/8—20/9/58.**G.**

BOILERS:
7267.

7685 *(new)* 9/8/24.
7550 *(ex4631)* 23/7/27.
7456 *(ex4671)* 30/4/32.
8863 *(new)* 11/1/36.
8843 *(ex4653)* 2/4/38.
8980 *(ex4665)* 20/10/45.
9152 *(ex1763)* 22/5/47.
9151 *(ex61774)* 2/9/49.
9151 reno. 21188 23/8/51.
21185 *(new)* 9/5/53.
21176 *(ex61763)* 20/9/58.

SHEDS:
Ardsley.
March *after* 8/24.
Colwick 13/6/25
Stratford 1/7/25.
Southend ?/?
Stratford 30/11/29.
Southend 14/12/29.
Stratford 21/12/29.
March 26/2/40.
Norwich 22/6/47.
Stratford 17/10/47.
South Lynn 26/11/47.
March 26/10/52.
Lincoln 13/9/53.
Immingham 10/10/54.
Boston 7/11/54.
New England 8/1/61.

RENUMBERED:
4652 9/8/24.
1742 24/3/46.
61742 2/9/49.

CONDEMNED: 15/5/62.
Into Don. for cut up 15/5/62.

4653

Doncaster 1468.

To traffic 6/1916.

REPAIRS:
VcA. 24/2—1/9/21.**G.**
Don. 7/11/23—19/1/24.**G.**
As 1653N.
Altered to G.E. gauge.
Don. 29/12/25—26/3/26.**G.**
Str. ?/?—2/11/27.**N/C.**
Westinghouse brake fitted.
Don. 28/8—14/11/28.**G.**
Don. 3/1—7/2/31.**G.**
Don. 30/9—4/11/33.**G.**
Don. 11/5—8/6/35.**G.**
Don. 13/2—13/3/37.**G.**
Don. 27/11—11/12/37.**G.**
Don. 8—29/6/40.**G.**
Don. 29/8—3/10/42.**G.**
Cow. 23/12/44—10/2/45.**G.**
Cow. 12/3—15/5/47.**G.**
Cow. 23/9—25/10/47.**L.**
Cow. 27/4—29/5/48.**L.**

Cow. 26/1—11/3/50.**G.**
Cow. 15/7—1/9/51.**L/I.**
Cow. 11/10—21/11/53.**H/I.**
Cow. 17/11—17/12/55.**G.**
Cow. 21—24/12/55.**N/C.**
Cow. 17—21/1/56.**N/C.**

BOILERS:
7268.
7261 *(ex1650)* 19/1/24.
7461 *(ex4650)* 14/11/28.
8843 *(new)* 8/6/35.
9073 *(new)* 11/12/37.
8840 *(ex4687)* 3/10/42.
8560 *(ex1776)* 11/3/50.
8560 reno. 21110 1/9/51.
21122 *(ex61785)* 17/12/55.

SHEDS:
King's Cross.
Stratford 10/4/26.
Cambridge 7/1/27.
March 4/6/28.
Cambridge 23/7/28.
March 3/5/29.
Norwich 9/10/35.
March 7/11/35.
Norwich 22/6/47.
Stratford 17/10/47.
South Lynn 26/11/47.
March 2/11/51.
Lincoln 13/9/53.
Boston 13/2/55.

RENUMBERED:
4653 12/2/25.
1743 19/5/46.
61743 29/5/48.

CONDEMNED: 22/6/59.
Sold for scrap to Motherwell Machinery & Scrap, Wishaw, 28/10/59.

4654

Doncaster 1470.

To traffic 7/1916.

REPAIRS:
Don. 29/3—19/8/22.**G.**
Don. 30/10/24—21/3/25.**G.**
Don. 30/3—16/6/28.**G.**
Altered to G.E. gauge.
Don. 21/6—2/8/30.**G.**
Don. 20/8—8/10/32.**G.**
Don. 7/7—11/8/34.**G.**
Don. 21/3—25/4/36.**G.**
Don. 5/3—9/4/38.**G.**
Don. 18/5—15/6/40.**G.**
Don. 8/5—5/6/43.**G.**
Don. 10/2—3/3/45.**G.**
Cow. 16/1—15/3/47.**G.**
Cow. 7/12/49—21/1/50.**H/I.**

Cow. 11/9—6/10/50.**N/C.**
Cow. 2/1—18/2/52.**G.**
Cow. 16/2—17/3/55.**H/I.**
Cow. 22—24/3/55.**N/C.**

BOILERS:
7266.
7453 *(ex1662)* 21/3/25.
7267 *(ex4685)* 2/8/30.
8867 *(new)* 25/4/36.
9201 *(new)* 15/6/40.
8860 *(ex1759)* 15/3/47.
21129 *(ex61792)* 18/2/52.

SHEDS:
King's Cross.
Ardsley 21/2/25.
Brunswick 4/12/25.
New England 12/2/27.
Colwick 31/7/30.
New England 25/9/30.
Boston 24/6/33.
New England 31/8/33.
Boston 21/6/40.
New England 16/4/45.
Boston 16/6/46.

RENUMBERED:
4654 21/3/25.
1744 20/5/46.
61744 21/1/50.

CONDEMNED: 7/1/57.

4655

Doncaster 1471.

To traffic 10/1916.

REPAIRS:
Don. 2/11/21—18/3/22.**G.**
Don. 27/11/24—14/3/25.**G.**
Don. 3/12/25—2/1/26.**L.**
Don. 7/12/26—26/3/27.**G.**
Altered to G.E. gauge.
Don. 3/9—15/10/27.**L.**
Westinghouse brake fitted.
Don. 6/7—6/10/28.**G.**
Don. 18/10—22/11/30.**G.**
Don. 6/5—10/6/33.**G.**
Don. 16/2—23/3/35.**G.**
Don. 26/6—24/7/37.**G.**
Don. 3/2—2/3/40.**G.**
Don. 23/11—14/12/40.**L.**
Don. 5/9—10/10/42.**G.**
Cow. 14/3—29/4/44.**G.**
Cow. 17/8—16/9/44.**L.**
Cow. 15/12/44—26/1/45.**L.**
Don. 5/2—2/5/46.**G.**
Cow. 11/8—7/11/47.**G.**
Cow. 9/5—11/7/48.**L.**
Cow. 12/2—18/3/50.**L/I.**
Cow. 10/8—1/12/51.**G.**
Cow. 19/11—25/12/54.**G.**

(above) On the left side of boilers built from December 1934, three handholes were still provided for washing out purposes.

(right) Engines allocated to Eastfield shed were fitted with drop grates from December 1933 so as to use the wet ash pit at that depot. By February 1936 Nos.4674, 4682, 4684, 4685, 4691, 4692, 4693, 4697, 4698, 4699, 4700, 4701 and 4704 had been equipped. Two more were similarly fitted in BR days, to 61784 in October 1948 and 61786 in December 1949. The operating rod was on the left hand side at an angle from the cab to the bottom of the firebox. Note tender has three coal rails.

All were built to GN gauge with heights from rail at 13ft 4in. for the chimney and dome, and 13ft 4⅝in. to the top of the whistle which was mounted on the cab roof. To the top of the Ramsbottom safety valves was 13ft 0⅞in.

The last twenty-five had Ross 'Pop' valves and their height from rail was only 12ft 6⅝in. but the whistle was still on the top of the cab at 13ft 4⅝in. On GN Section workings and on NE lines to York and Hull these heights did not pose a problem.

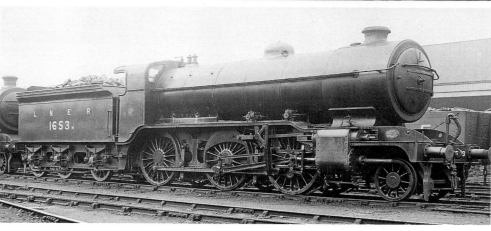

In November 1923 drawings were prepared for alterations to enable K2 class to work on the GE and NB sections where the gauge was less generous. The first two to be altered were ex works 8th December 1923 (No.1674N) and 19th January 1924 (No.1653N) and had 1ft 2in. chimneys which cut their height there to 12ft 10½in. The regulator in the dome was modified to allow a flatter and 2¾in. shorter dome casing to be used. Ross 'Pops' replaced Ramsbottom safety valves but on a special seating where a boiler had been drilled for Ramsbottom valves. The cab was cut by 3in. and the whistle was moved from the top to the front of the cab to give 12ft 10in. from rail level.

During 1924, nine more were cut down and the five with boilers drilled for Ramsbottom valves and needing special seating were: 4644 (5/7/24), 4652 (9/8/24), 4656 (16/8/24), 4631 (20/9/24) and 4647 (4/10/24). All these five then went to GE Section sheds.

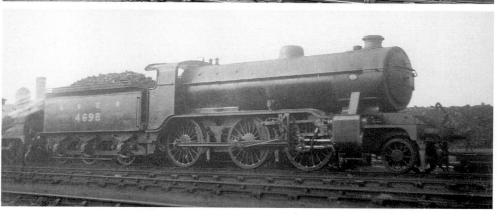

The other four cut down in 1924 already had Ross 'Pop' safety valves from new, Nos.4698 (5/7/24), 4695 (12/7/24), 4700 (16/8/24) and 4704 (27/9/24). These remained at GN sheds whilst negotiations proceeded with Scottish Area but on 22nd December 1924 all four went to Eastfield.

Cow. 11—29/1/55.**N/C**.
Cow. 19/9—19/10/57.**H/I**.

BOILERS:
　7264.
　7465 *(ex1674)* 26/3/27.
　7602 *(ex4681)* 6/10/28.
　8825 *(new)* 23/3/35.
　9197 *(new)* 2/3/40.
　9346 *(new)* 10/10/42.
　9008 *(ex4666)* 29/4/44.
　9345 *(ex4664)* 2/5/46.
　8981 *(ex1741)* 7/11/47.
　21138 *(ex61788)* 1/12/51.
　21162 *(ex61759)* 25/12/54.

SHEDS:
　King's Cross.
　Doncaster 29/10/25.
　Cambridge 20/10/27.
　Stratford 12/1/28.
　Yarmouth 10/10/28.
　Norwich 31/12/28
　March 3/3/30.
　Norwich 17/10/35.
　Lowestoft 5/11/39.
　Norwich 10/12/39.
　March 25/5/44.
　Norwich 6/12/46.
　Lowestoft 26/3/47.
　Stratford 22/10/47.
　Lincoln 5/10/52.
　Boston 15/3/53.
　Immingham 1/3/59.

RENUMBERED:
　4655 14/3/25.
　1745 29/12/46.
　61745 11/7/48.

CONDEMNED: 25/11/60.
Into Don. for cut up 25/11/60.

4656

Doncaster 1472.

To traffic 11/1916.

REPAIRS:
Don. 22/7—22/10/21.**G**.
Don. 12/3—16/8/24.**G**.
Altered to G.E. gauge.
Don. 14/5—21/9/27.**G**.
Westinghouse brake fitted.
Don. 5/7—16/8/30.**G**.
Don. 11/11—9/12/33.**G**.
Don. 9/5—13/6/36.**G**.
Str. 17—24/7/37.**L**.
Don. 23/4—14/5/38.**G**.
Don. 3/8—21/9/40.**G**.
Don. 7/11—12/12/42.**G**.
Cow. 5/4—5/5/45.**G**.
Cow. 18/5—12/10/47.**G**.
Cow. 18/7—26/11/49.**H/I**.

Cow. 1/11—28/12/51.**G**.
Cow. 20/4—21/5/55.**L/I**.
Cow. 23—28/5/55.**N/C**.
Cow. 1—24/7/55.**N/C**.
Dar. 18/2/59. *Not repaired.*

BOILERS:
　7265.
　7686 *(new)* 16/8/24.
　7609 *(ex4688)* 16/8/30.
　7942 *(ex4678)* 14/5/38.
　9197 *(ex4655)* 12/12/42.
　8826 *(ex4631)* 5/5/45.
　21140 *(ex61745)* 28/12/51.

SHEDS:
　King's Cross.
　Stratford 28/8/25.
　Cambridge 4/1/27.
　March 15/3/39.
　Norwich 5/4/46.
　Stratford 22/10/47.
　Lincoln 5/10/52.
　Boston 29/12/57.

RENUMBERED:
　4656 16/8/24.
　1746 29/7/46.
　61746 26/11/49.

CONDEMNED: 27/2/59.
Cut up at Darlington.

4657

Doncaster 1473.

To traffic 11/1916.

REPAIRS:
Don. 21/9/21—14/1/22.**G**.
Don. 16—23/9/22.**L**.
Don. 11/1—17/5/24.**G**.
Don. 13/9—27/12/26.**G**.
Don. 22/10—3/12/27.**L**.
Don. 2/11/28—17/1/29.**G**.
Don. 3/5—14/6/30.**G**.
Don. 6/8—17/9/32.**G**.
Don. 10/11—8/12/34.**G**.
Don. 23/5—27/6/36.**G**.
Don. 16/7—13/8/38.**G**.
Don. 20/7—24/8/40.**G**.
Don. 11/10—6/12/41.**G**.
Don. 18—25/4/42.**L**.
Cow. 20/2—25/3/44.**G**.
Cow. 13/7—24/8/46.**G**.
Don. 15/10/46—8/2/47.**L**.
Cow. 20/10/48—8/1/49.**G**.
Cow. 28/4—5/6/52.**L/I**.
Gor. 21/11/52—10/1/53.**C/L**.
Gor. 13—17/1/53.**N/C**.
Gor. 19/10—28/11/53.**C/L**.
Cow. 24/3—15/5/54.**G**.
Cow. 18/1—22/2/58.**H/I**.

BOILERS:
　7262.
　7257 *(ex1645)* 14/1/22.
　7607 *(ex4643)* 17/1/29.
　7550 *(ex4652)* 17/9/32.
　7549 *(ex4668)* 8/12/34.
　8979 *(ex4688)* 13/8/38.
　C1827 *(ex4695)* 25/3/44.
　9200 *(ex1758)* 8/1/49.
　9200 reno. 21163 5/6/52.
　21113 *(ex61777)* 15/5/54.

SHEDS:
　Doncaster.
　Ardsley 26/2/25.
　Copley Hill ?/?
　Doncaster 21/2/28.
　Copley Hill 21/9/32.
　King's Cross 2/10/33.
　New England 31/10/33.
　Boston 14/6/40.
　New England 14/7/40.
　Yarmouth 15/10/50.
　Norwich 17/12/50.
　Colwick 11/3/51.
　Darnall 26/6/55.

RENUMBERED:
　4657 17/5/24.
　1747 23/8/46.
　61747 8/1/49.

CONDEMNED: 5/12/60.
Into Don. for cut up 5/12/60.

4658

Doncaster 1474.

To traffic 12/1916.

REPAIRS:
Don. 22/3—9/7/21.**G**.
Don. 17/12/23—10/5/24.**G**.
Don. 29/4—20/9/26.**G**.
Don. 4/7—31/8/28.**G**.
Don. 22/2—22/3/30.**G**.
Don. 31/12/31—30/1/32.**G**.
Don. 10/2—10/3/34.**G**.
Don. 2—30/11/35.**G**.
Don. 8/5—5/6/37.**G**.
Don. 22/4—10/6/39.**G**.
Don. 16/12/39—16/3/40.**L**.
Don. 21/9—7/12/40.**L**.
Don. 7/2—14/3/42.**G**.
Don. 26/6—31/7/43.**L**.
Don. 25/12/43—8/1/44.**L**.
Cow. 1/10—2/11/44.**G**.
Cow. 25/10/46—16/3/47.**G**.
Don. 12/3—30/4/48.**G**.
Cow. 9/3—1/4/50.**H/I**.
Cow. 12/8—29/9/52.**G**.
Cow. 30/9—19/11/55.**H/I**.

BOILERS:
　7269.
　7549 *(new)* 9/7/21.
　7457 *(ex4666)* 31/8/28.
　7601 *(ex4680)* 22/3/30.
　8861 *(new)* 30/11/35.
　8825 *(ex4655)* 14/3/42.
　9154 *(ex4689)* 2/11/44.
　21182 *(new)* 29/9/52.

SHEDS:
　Ardsley.
　Doncaster 21/2/28.
　Boston 8/7/34.
　Doncaster 23/8/34.
　March 15/10/37.
　Norwich 13/1/46.
　Lowestoft 26/3/47.
　Stratford 13/10/47.
　South Lynn 26/11/47.
　Lincoln 13/9/53.
　Boston 10/7/55.

RENUMBERED:
　4658 10/5/24.
　1748 17/11/46.
　61748 30/4/48.

CONDEMNED: 22/6/59.
Sold for scrap to Motherwell
Machinery & Scrap, Wishaw,
30/11/59.

4659

Doncaster 1475.

To traffic 12/1916.

REPAIRS:
Don. 25/1—17/6/22.**G**.
Don. 30/10/24—14/2/25.**G**.
Don. 25/4—16/7/27.**G**.
Don. 26/1—23/3/29.**G**.
Don. 12/7—16/8/30.**G**.
Don. 4/6—27/8/32.**G**.
Don. 24/11—22/12/34.**G**.
Don. 18/7—15/8/36.**G**.
Don. 11/12—31/12/37.**G**.
Don. 9—30/4/38.**L**.
Don. 22/6—13/7/40.**G**.
Don. 1—29/5/43.**G**.
Cow. 28/8—29/9/45.**G**.
Don. 22/6—7/9/46.**G**.
Cow. 24/11/47—30/1/48.**G**.
Cow. 16/2—26/3/49.**H/I**.
Cow. 21/11—24/12/49.**C/H**.
Cow. 10/8—22/12/51.**G**.
Cow. 27/9—24/10/53.**G**.
Cow. 3/2—12/3/55.**C/H**.
Cow. 24/10—24/11/56.**H/I**.
Cow. 11/10—9/11/57.**C/L**.

BOILERS:
　7300.

7625 (ex4673) 16/7/27.
7468 (ex4678) 23/3/29.
8823 (new) 22/12/34.
8867 (ex4654) 13/7/40.
8982 (ex4632) 29/9/45.
9011 (ex1739) 30/1/48.
8866 (ex1729) 24/12/49.
8866 reno. 21132 22/12/51.
21168 (ex61750) 24/10/53.

SHEDS:
Doncaster.
New England ?/?
Ardsley 19/2/25.
Doncaster 21/7/27.
Colwick 25/8/30.
Doncaster 27/7/32.
Copley Hill 22/9/32.
Colwick 21/5/33.
King's Cross 6/10/33.
Colwick 2/11/33.
Boston 18/6/36.
New England 22/9/36.
Boston 8/10/41.
Colwick 16/4/45.
Darnall 26/6/55.
Colwick 2/6/57.

RENUMBERED:
4659 14/2/25.
1749 4/8/46.
61749 26/3/49.

CONDEMNED: 27/1/59.
Into Dar. for cut up 18/4/59.

4660

N.B.L. Co. 21971.

To traffic 6/1918.

REPAIRS:
Don. 31/5—7/10/22.**G.**
Don. 11/8/24—17/1/25.**G.**
Don. 13—25/8/25.**L.**
Don. 2/3—22/7/26.**G.**
Don. 4—18/8/26.**L.**
Don. 23/4—24/6/27.**L.**
Don. 24/3—16/6/28.**G.**
Altered to G.E. gauge.
Don. 28/11/28—2/2/29.**G.**
Don. 26/4—31/5/30.**G.**
Don. 31/12/31—13/2/32.**G.**
Don. 31/3—21/4/34.**G.**
Don. 16/11—14/12/35.**G.**
Don. 20/3—17/4/37.**G.**
Don. 5—19/11/38.**G.**
Don. 27/7—31/8/40.**G.**
Don. 30/11/40—11/1/41.**L.**
Don. 22/8—26/9/42.**G.**

Don. 19/12/42—9/1/43.**L.**
Don. 25/9—30/10/43.**L.**
Cow. 21/2—8/4/44.**G.**
Cow. 26/2—21/3/45.**L.**
Cow. 21/10—28/12/46.**G.**
Cow. 1/10—17/12/48.**G.**
Cow. 14/9—28/10/50.**H/I.**
Cow. 6/9—10/1/53.**G.**
Cow. 23—30/1/53.**N/C.**
Cow. 28/8—24/9/55.**G.**
Cow. 3—5/10/55.**N/C.**

BOILERS:
7451.
7252 (ex1643) 17/1/25.
7260 (ex4671) 2/2/29.
8559 (new) 21/4/34.
9152 (new) 19/11/38.
9349 (new) 8/4/44.
C1786 (ex1775) 28/12/46.
9346 (ex1767) 17/12/48.
21118 (ex61734) 10/1/53.
21144 (ex61738) 24/9/55.

SHEDS:
New England.
Doncaster ?/?
Colwick 1/1/35.
Boston 5/7/35.
Colwick 10/9/35.
Boston 8/1/50.

RENUMBERED:
4660 17/1/25.
1750 6/10/46.
61750 17/12/48.

CONDEMNED: 22/6/59.
Sold for scrap to Motherwell
Machinery & Scrap, Wishaw,
28/10/59.

4661

N.B.L. Co. 21972.

To traffic 6/1918.

REPAIRS:
Don. 31/5—7/10/22.**G.**
Don. 13/8—12/12/24.**G.**
Don. 21/10/26—18/1/27.**G.**
Don. 13/9—15/11/28.**G.**
Don. 29/3—3/5/30.**G.**
Don. 7/11—19/12/31.**G.**
Don. 30/12/33—3/2/34.**G.**
Don. 13/4—11/5/35.**G.**
Don. 20/2—20/3/37.**G.**
Don. 15/4—27/5/39.**G.**
Don. 1—29/11/41.**G.**
Don. 29/8/42.**L.**

Cow. 16/2—8/4/44.**G.**
Cow. 21/3—7/4/45.**L.**
Cow. 19/12/45—2/2/46.**L.**
Cow. 17/7—10/10/47.**G.**
Cow. 16/1—3/3/50.**G.**
Cow. 12/5—15/7/52.**G.**
Cow. 12/11—19/12/52.**C/L.**
Cow. 15/11—4/12/54.**G.**
Cow. 8—11/12/54.**N/C.**
Cow. 29—31/12/54.**N/C.**

BOILERS:
7452.
7470 (ex4679) 18/1/27.
7603 (ex4682) 15/11/28.
7256 (ex4655) 19/12/31.
8558 (new) 3/2/34.
9348 (new) 8/4/44.
7624 (ex1752) 10/10/47.
8759 (ex61791) 3/3/50.
8759 reno. 21114 15/7/52.
21128 (ex61756) 4/12/54.

SHEDS:
New England.
Doncaster ?/?
Colwick 1/1/35.
March 4/7/35.
Norwich 14/10/35.
Bradford 9/2/36.
Copley Hill 2/12/36.
Ardsley 30/7/39.
New England 23/2/40.
Doncaster 8/4/42.
Colwick 23/8/46.
Lincoln 17/6/56.
Boston 23/2/58.

RENUMBERED:
4661 12/12/24.
1751 8/9/46.
61751 3/3/50.

CONDEMNED: 22/6/59.
Sold for scrap to Motherwell
Machinery & Scrap, Wishaw,
30/11/59.

4662

N.B.L. Co. 21973.

To traffic 6/1918.

REPAIRS:
Don. 1/3—22/7/22.**G.**
Don. 12/8/24—14/2/25.**G.**
Don. 15/10/26—10/3/27.**G.**
Don. 3/9—1/10/27.**L.**
Altered to G.E. gauge.
Westinghouse brake fitted.

Don. 16/3—4/5/29.**G.**
Don. 17/10—14/11/31.**G.**
Don. 17/11/34—5/1/35.**G.**
Don. 19/9—17/10/36.**G.**
Don. 13/3—24/4/37.**L.**
Don. 25/3—27/5/39.**G.**
Don. 21/6—19/7/41.**G.**
Don. 20/2—20/3/43.**G.**
Cow. 8/8—15/9/45.**G.**
Cow. 18/5—10/9/47.**G.**
Cow. 22/10—14/11/47.**L.**
Cow. 20/6—9/9/50.**G.**
Cow. 9—30/5/53.**L/I.**
Westinghouse brake removed.
Cow. 11/1—6/3/54.**C/L.**
Cow. 7/9—5/11/55.**G.**
Cow. 24/2—31/3/56.**C/L.**

BOILERS:
7453.
7269 (ex1673) 14/2/25.
7611 (ex4669) 14/11/31.
9192 (new) 27/5/39.
7624 (ex4686) 15/9/45.
8862 (ex1757) 10/9/47.
8840 (ex61743) 9/9/50.
8840 reno.21120 30/5/53.
21166 (ex61775) 5/11/55.

SHEDS:
New England.
Doncaster ?/?
Ardsley 21/2/25.
Stratford 6/10/27.
Southend 30/11/29.
Stratford 14/12/29.
Southend 14/6/30.
Stratford 21/6/30.
March 25/4/40.
Norwich 13/1/46.
Stratford 17/10/47.
Colwick 5/10/52.

RENUMBERED:
4662 14/2/25.
1752 31/3/46.
61752 9/9/50.

CONDEMNED: 11/12/59.
Into Str. for cut up 1/60.

4663

N.B.L. Co. 21974.

To traffic 7/1918.

REPAIRS:
Don. 1/7—21/10/22.**G.**
Don. 28/9—20/12/24.**G.**
Don. 10/2—12/5/27.**L.**

WORKS CODES:- Cw - Cowlairs. Dar- Darlington. Dfu - Dunfermline shed. Don - Doncaster. Etfd - Eastfied shed. Ghd - Gateshead. Gor - Gorton. Inv - Inverurie.
ThJ - Thornton Junction shed. Str - Stratford. VcA - Vickers Armstrong.
REPAIR CODES:- **C/H** - Casual Heavy. **C/L** - Casual Light. **G** - General. **H** - Heavy. **H/I** - Heavy Intermediate. **L** - Light. **L/I** - Light Intermediate. **N/C** - Non-Classified.

Scottish Area found the K2 so acceptable that ten more were cut down and sent: 4691 (18/2/25), 4692 (21/3/25), 4693 (20/6/25), 4694 (30/5/25), 4696 (27/2/25), 4697 (18/3/25), 4699 (28/3/25), 4701 (4/3/25), 4702 (13/6/25) and 4703 (13/6/25). All these already had Ross 'Pop' safety valves. Note that twin irons for redundant London Area lamp codes were not taken off.

When the Scottish Area needed six more from late 1931, some cut-down engines were already available; those transferred were 4674 (11/12/31), 4682 (29/10/31), 4684 (17/11/31), 4685 (30/10/31), 4686 (25/1/32) and 4689 (7/1/32). Note 12in. LNER put on as standard by Doncaster 17/10/31 and which Cowlairs changed to 7½in. by December 1933.

At least one Scottish Area engine retained its whistle above the cab roof. With cab height cut to 12ft 3in. and the whistle on a short stem, it was still well within the permissible 13ft 0in. Only No.4703 was so observed. Even the change to side window cab did not affect 4703's singular whistle position and it was still above the cab roof when renumbered to 1793 on 3rd February 1946. Ex works on 12th January 1952, the whistle had been moved to the front of the cab.

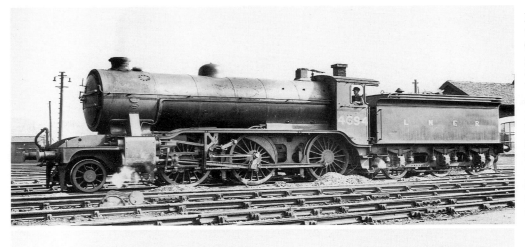

Boilers with Ramsbottom safety valves had a height there of 13ft 0¾in. and were strictly out of gauge on NB and GE lines but odd ones must have been tolerated. When Nos.4682 and 4689 were cut down in October and December 1931 to go to Scottish Area, Doncaster did not change the safety valves and so these boilers kept their Ramsbottom type valves. That from 4682 was used by 4695 (5/33 to 5/36) and by 4694 (6/36 to 11/41). 4689's boiler later went on 4704 from 2/36 to 3/40.

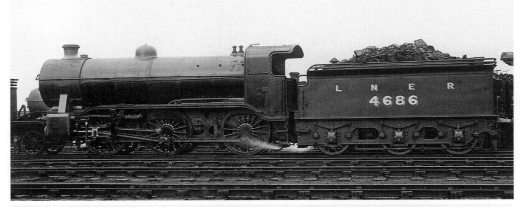

Various combinations of chimney and safety valves could be seen. Ex works 26th March 1925, No.4686 still had original tall chimney and dome but the boiler had been changed to that built for No.4652 and 'Pops' had replaced Ramsbottom. The whistle had also been moved from above to front of the cab.

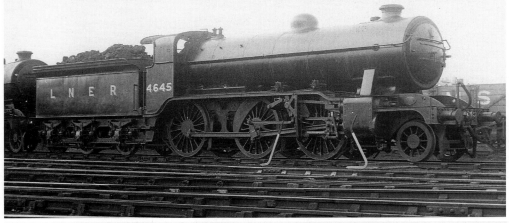

From 6th August 1927 to 18th July 1936, No.4645 carried two of the last batch of boilers drilled for Ramsbottom safety valves but on which 'Pops' had been mounted. Here it has short chimney, but original dome. Gauge restrictions were not applicable because until February 1940 No.4645 did all its work from King's Cross shed.

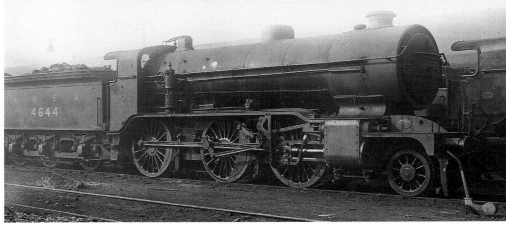

No.4644 was cut below 13ft 0in. ex works 5th July 1924 but on 4th January 1929 the boiler had been changed to one still with Ramsbottom safety valves. As these were out of gauge, GE Section immediately transferred it to King's Cross shed. It returned to GE in 1932 but by then had 'Pops'.

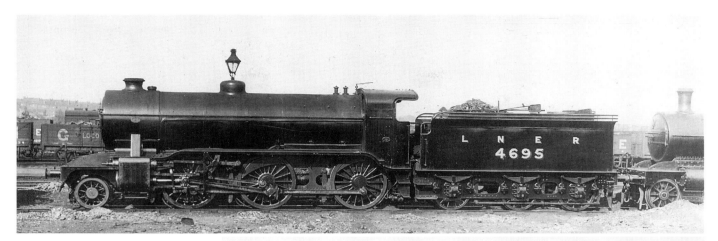

(above) **No.4695** got its cut-down chimney, dome and cab ex works 12th July 1924 but did not leave the GN Section until 22nd December. As built it had Ross 'Pops' mounted directly on the firebox.

(right) In 1927 No.4646's original boiler was sent to Cowlairs to provide a spare and cut repair times. It was first used by No.4703, ex works 29th October 1927 to January 1932, and then from 25th March 1933 on 4693. It had 'Pops' on Ramsbottom mounting but no cover around their base.

Off No.4693 in February 1938, the above boiler went to No.4689, ex works 25th August 1938, when Cowlairs had made a definitely different shape of cover for the base of the safety valves. Note Class K.2 now on the buffer beam.

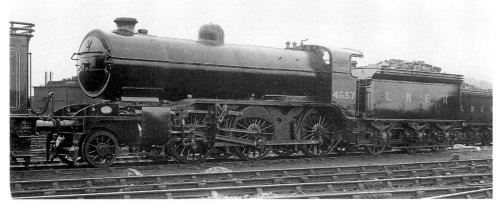

No.4657 worked entirely on the GN Section until 1950 and so was unaffected by gauge restrictions. During 1927-29 the whole class were brought within 13ft 1in. maximum height, but ex works 8th December 1934 it had a high dome which never belonged to any variety of K2 class.

Ex Cowlairs 27th June 1939, No.4702 had been fitted with this flat-top dome cover which it then kept to its 2nd September 1960 withdrawal. As 61792 it was ex works 17th July 1948 with this straight sided chimney akin to the type used on N2 class. During the 1950's it reverted to normal chimney.

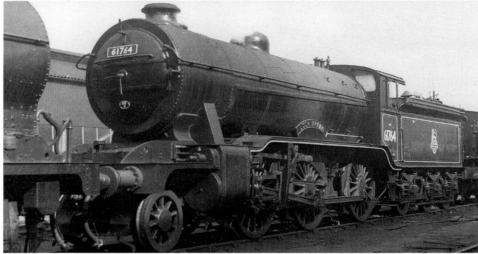

By its June 1954 shopping, No.61764 had this same or a similar straight sided chimney; these two, Nos.61764 and 61792 being the only ones seen so fitted. 61764 then kept this chimney to withdrawal.

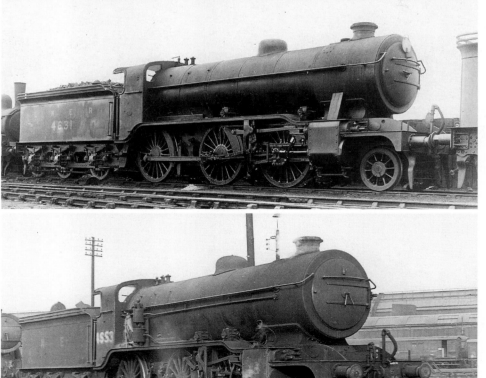

Nos.4630 to 4659 at first had cylinders with their live steam pipes out of sight between the frames, but from 1925, as renewals were required, the later pattern with outside steam pipes was fitted, No.4631 getting them ex works 1st October 1926.

The original pattern cylinders could still be seen to the end of the LNER, No.4653 still being so fitted until it went to works on 12th March 1947.

Westinghouse pump only fitted.
Don. 8—19/10/27.**L.**
Altered to G.E. gauge.
Westinghouse brake completed.
Don. 8/11/28—19/1/29.**G.**
Don. 15/2—29/3/30.**G.**
Don. 12/3—23/4/32.**G.**
Don. 19/5—23/6/34.**G.**
Don. 14/3—4/4/36.**G.**
Don. 25/12/37—8/1/38.**G.**
Don. 22/4—3/6/39.**G.**
Don. 12/9—10/10/42.**G.**
Cow. 25/6—5/8/44.**G.**
Cow. 23/5—10/7/45.**G.**
Don. 6/9—27/10/46.**L.**
Cow. 24/3—19/7/47.**G.**
Cow. 23/9—12/10/47.**L.**
Don. 15/1—20/2/48.**L.**
Cow. 21/7—27/8/49.**H/I.**
Cow. 4/7—20/9/51.**G.**
Cow. 16/2—20/3/54.**H/I.**
Cow. 25/4—2/6/55.**G.**

BOILERS:
7454.
7610 (ex4689) 19/1/29.
7258 (ex4680) 23/4/32.
8561 (new) 23/6/34.
8862 (ex4639) 8/1/38.
9193 (new) 3/6/39.
9009 (ex4636) 10/7/45.
8869 (ex1755) 19/7/47.
21165 (ex61723) 20/9/51.
21171 (ex61769) 2/6/55.

SHEDS:
New England.
Ardsley ?/?
Stratford 3/11/27.
Cambridge 18/1/29.
New England 5/3/29.
March 17/10/29.
New England 31/12/29.
Norwich 24/9/30.
Lowestoft 4/10/30.
New England 9/1/31.
Norwich 6/8/32.
Lowestoft 2/10/32.
Norwich 15/1/33.
Lowestoft 6/10/34.
Norwich 3/11/34.
Yarmouth 21/11/34.
Norwich 15/12/34.
Lowestoft 5/10/35.
Norwich 17/12/35.
Lowestoft 4/10/36.
Norwich 24/1/37.
March 22/2/45.
Norwich 13/1/46.
Stratford 22/10/47.
Colwick 5/10/52.

RENUMBERED:
4663 20/12/24.
1753 13/10/46.

E1753 20/2/48.
61753 27/8/49.

CONDEMNED: 28/9/59.
Sold for scrap to Motherwell Machinery & Scrap, Wishaw, 2/60.

4664

N.B.L. Co. 21975.

To traffic 7/1918.

REPAIRS:
Don. 15/11/22—7/5/23.**G.**
Don. 6/2—9/5/25.**G.**
Don. 15/1—11/6/27.**G.**
Altered to G.E. gauge.
Westinghouse brake fitted.
Don. 31/8—5/10/29.**G.**
Front end heating apparatus fitted.
Don. 27/2—2/4/32.**G.**
Don. 4/10—3/11/34.**G.**
Don. 3—24/7/37.**G.**
Don. 2/12/39—6/1/40.**G.**
Don. 3—31/10/42.**G.**
Don. 30/1—20/2/43.**L.**
Cow. 10/11/43—22/1/44.**G.**
Don. 3/3—18/4/46.**G.**
Cow. 13/4—8/5/47.**L.**
Don. 27/2—7/4/48.**G.**
Cow. 6/7—24/8/50.**H/I.**
Cow. 6—7/9/50.**N/C.**
Cow. 23/6—27/8/52.**G.**
Cow. 15/5—19/6/54.**L/I.**
Cow. 3/5—16/6/56.**G.**

BOILERS:
7455.
7266 (ex1654) 9/5/25.
7840 (new) 11/6/27.
7839 (ex4635) 2/4/32.
9011 (new) 24/7/37.
9073 (ex4653) 31/10/42.
9345 (new) 22/1/44.
9472 (new) 18/4/46.
21179 (new) 27/8/52.
21110 (ex61743) 16/6/56.

SHEDS:
New England.
Annesley 28/5/25.
Doncaster 1/1/27.
New England 8/1/27.
Stratford 25/7/27.
Yarmouth 12/10/29.
Stratford 31/12/29.
Norwich 10/5/32.
Yarmouth 9/10/32.
Norwich 5/8/33.
Yarmouth 5/10/35.
Norwich 17/12/35.
Yarmouth 4/10/36.

Norwich 24/1/37.
March 23/5/44.
Norwich 13/1/46.
Lowestoft 26/3/47.
Stratford 17/10/47.
Colwick 5/10/52.

RENUMBERED:
4664 9/5/25.
1754 13/10/46.
61754 7/4/48.

CONDEMNED: 30/12/59.
Into Str. for cut up 1/60.

4665

N.B.L. Co. 21976.

To traffic 7/1918.

REPAIRS:
Don. 15/2—10/6/22.**G.**
Don. 28/8—31/12/24.**G.**
Don. 3/3—18/6/27.**G.**
Don. 27/4—1/6/29.**G.**
Don. 13/12/30—31/1/31.**G.**
Don. 22/4—3/6/33.**G.**
Don. 4/5—1/6/35.**G.**
Don. 16/1—6/2/37.**G.**
Don. 14/1—11/2/39.**G.**
Don. 14/12/40—18/1/41.**G.**
Don. 31/7—28/8/43.**G.**
Cow. 23/7—1/9/45.**G.**
Cow. ?/?—6/2/47.**C/H.**
Cow. 11/10—27/11/47.**G.**
Cow. ?/?—1/5/48.**L.**
Cow. ?/?—?/10/49.**C/L.**
Cow. 7/1—10/2/51.**G.**
Cow. 2—22/8/53.**H/I.**
ThJ. 1—12/6/54.**C/L.**
ThJ. 11—19/11/55.**C/L.**
Cow. 8/3—21/4/56.**G.**
WPU gear removed.
Cow. 19/11—14/12/57.**H/I.**

BOILERS:
7456.
7256 (ex4642) 18/6/27.
7687 (ex4675) 31/1/31.
7837 (ex4631) 3/6/33.
8757 (ex4690) 11/2/39.
8980 (ex4632) 28/8/43.
8869 (ex4639) 1/9/45.
7616 (ex1756) 6/2/47.
21127 (ex1752) 10/2/51.
21100 (ex61722) 21/4/56.

SHEDS:
New England.
Annesley 28/5/25.
Doncaster 7/1/27.
March 22/6/31.
Doncaster 19/8/31.
New England 7/12/37.

Boston 8/10/41.
Colwick 16/4/45.
Boston 2/7/46.
Eastfield 11/2/51.
Thornton Jct 9/1/52.
Kittybrewster 19/2/57.
Keith 4/3/57.

RENUMBERED:
4665 31/12/24.
1755 10/11/46.
61755 1/5/48.

CONDEMNED: 18/11/59.
Sold for scrap to Motherwell Machinery & Scrap, Wishaw, 14/3/60.

4666

N.B.L. Co. 21977.

To traffic 7/1918.

REPAIRS:
Don. 7—19/11/21.**G.**
Don. 9/1—5/5/23.**G.**
Don. 19/5—19/9/25.**G.**
Don. 12—23/1/26.**L.**
Don. 8/7—8/10/27.**G.**
Altered to G.E. gauge.
Don. 21/9—23/11/28.**G.**
Don. 9/11—21/12/29.**G.**
Don. 21/3—25/4/31.**G.**
Don. 18/3—13/5/33.**G.**
Don. 16/2—9/3/35.**G.**
Don. 20/3—24/4/37.**G.**
Don. 14/10—18/11/39.**G.**
Don. 4/4—2/5/42.**G.**
Cow. 20/2—1/4/44.**G.**
Cow. 3/10—10/11/45.**L.**
Cow. 19/9—11/1/47.**G.**
Cow. 14/9—11/12/48.**G.**
Cow. 3—23/6/51.**L/I.**
Cow. 12/10—4/12/51.**C/L.**
Cow. 28/10—6/12/52.**C/L.**
Cow. 1/4—26/6/54.**G.**
Cow. 30/6—3/9/55.**C/L.**
Cow. 13/6—10/8/57.**H/I.**
Cow. 6/11—14/12/57.**C/L.**
Cow. 29/8—4/10/58.**G.**

BOILERS:
7457.
7452 (ex4661) 8/10/27.
7265 (ex4670) 23/11/28.
7686 (ex4656) 25/4/31.
7546 (ex4667) 13/5/33.
9008 (ex4676) 18/11/39.
7616 (ex4682) 1/4/44.
C1828 (ex1794) 11/1/47.
8842 (ex1770) 11/12/48.
8842 reno. 21128 23/6/51.
21161 (ex61758) 26/6/54.
21186 (ex61733) 4/10/58.

SHEDS:
King's Cross.
Doncaster 30/10/25.
March 22/6/31.
Doncaster 9/9/31.
Boston 24/6/33.
Doncaster 25/8/33.
Boston 3/7/35.
Colwick 9/9/35.
Bradford 12/2/36.
Ardsley 25/1/40.
New England 23/2/40.
Colwick 18/8/46.
Boston 8/1/50.
Immingham 1/3/59.
Colwick 12/6/60.
King's Cross 29/1/61.

RENUMBERED:
4666 21/2/25.
1756 6/10/46.
61756 11/12/48.

CONDEMNED: 22/6/62.
Into Don. for cut up 22/6/62.

4667

N.B.L. Co. 21978.

To traffic 8/1918.

REPAIRS:
Don. 13—22/10/21.**G.**
Don. 11/4—18/8/23.**G.**
Don. 10/8—7/11/25.**G.**
Don. 1/10—16/11/27.**G.**
Don. 16/3—5/4/28.**L.**
*Westinghouse brake & front
heater connection fitted.*
Don. 8/2—8/3/30.**G.**
Don. 18/6—16/7/32.**G.**
Str. 11—23/5/33.**L.**
Don. 4/5—1/6/35.**G.**
Don. 12/11—3/12/38.**G.**
Don. 15/2—15/3/41.**G.**
Don. 21/2—11/4/42.**L.**
Don. 24/7—28/8/43.**G.**
Don. 30/12/44—27/1/45.**G.**
Cow. 11/3—15/8/47.**G.**
Cow. 2/1—14/2/48.**L.**
Cow. 27/8—30/10/48.**L.**
Cow. 31/1—18/3/50.**G.**
Str. 27/3—10/4/52.**N/C.**
Cow. 26/3—22/4/53.**H/I.**
Cow. 9/1—23/4/55.**G.**
Dar. 5/2/59. *Not repaired.*

BOILERS:
7458.
7546 *(ex4635)* 16/11/27.
7838 *(ex4684)* 16/7/32.
8841 *(new)* 1/6/35.
8862 *(ex4669)* 28/8/43.
8559 *(ex1726)* 15/8/47.

8824 *(ex61784)* 18/3/50.
8824 reno. 21117 22/4/53.
21114 *(ex61751)* 23/4/55.

SHEDS:
King's Cross.
Cambridge 14/4/28.
March 2/5/29.
Colchester 19/2/33.
Parkeston 26/3/34.
Colchester 19/11/35.
Norwich 6/2/36.
Yarmouth 22/10/39.
Lowestoft 7/12/39.
Norwich 21/1/40.
March 24/2/40.
Colchester 11/1/46.
South Lynn 6/4/48.
March 12/9/51.
Boston 29/6/52.

RENUMBERED:
4667 21/2/25.
1757 17/10/46.
61757 30/10/48.

CONDEMNED: 24/2/59.
Cut up at Darlington.

4668

N.B.L. Co. 21979.

To traffic 8/1918.

REPAIRS:
Don. 15—29/10/21.**G.**
Don. 5/4—11/8/23.**G.**
Don. 13/10—14/11/24.**L.**
Don. 21/6—9/10/26.**G.**
Don. 20/7—27/8/27.**L.**
Don. 4/10—17/11/28.**G.**
Don. 26/7—30/8/30.**G.**
Don. 27/8—1/10/32.**G.**
Don. 1/9—6/10/34.**G.**
Don. 22/8—26/9/36.**G.**
Don. 5/8—16/9/39.**G.**
Don. 8/11—6/12/41.**G.**
Don. 14/8—18/9/43.**G.**
Cow. 15/3—14/4/45.**G.**
Cow. 5—29/10/45.**C/H.**
Cow. ?/?—22/2/47.**C/L.**
Cow. 30/3—21/5/48.**G.**
Cow. 23/4—10/5/49.**N/C.**
Cow. 4/2—10/3/50.**L/I.**
Cow. 21/1—31/3/51.**H/I.**
Cow. 21—23/8/51.**C/L.**
Cow. 12/9—11/10/52.**H/I.**
New cab side window.
Cow. 22/2—27/3/54.**G.**
Cow. 20—26/4/54.**N/C.**
Cow. 16/5—16/6/56.**H/I.**
WPU gear removed.
Dfu. 16/8—5/9/57.**C/L.**

BOILERS:
7459.
7258 *(ex4647)* 9/10/26.
7452 *(ex4666)* 17/11/28.
7549 *(ex4674)* 1/10/32.
8760 *(new)* 6/10/34.
9195 *(new)* 16/9/39.
9200 *(ex4671)* 29/10/45.
9198 *(ex1781)* 21/5/48.
9198 reno. 21161 31/3/51.
21158 *(ex61730)* 27/3/54.

SHEDS:
King's Cross.
New England 29/2/40.
Doncaster 4/4/42.
Boston 7/4/46.
New England 16/6/46.
Colwick 18/8/46.
Eastfield 1/4/51.
Dunfermline 17/1/52

RENUMBERED:
4668 23/3/25.
1758 27/8/46.
61758 21/5/48.

CONDEMNED: 1/6/59.
*Sold for scrap to J.N.Connell,
Coatbridge, 28/7/59.*

4669

N.B.L. Co. 21980.

To traffic 8/1918.

REPAIRS:
Don. 15/10—5/11/21.**L.**
Don. 31/1—16/5/23.**G.**
Don. 17/9—28/11/25.**G.**
Don. 12/11/27—13/3/28.**G.**
Westinghouse brake fitted.
Don. 22/3—19/4/30.**G.**
Don. 21/10—25/11/33.**G.**
Don. 29/8—3/10/36.**G.**
Don. 5/11—3/12/38.**G.**
Don. 3—31/5/41.**G.**
Don. 21/3/42.**L.**
Don. 18—25/4/42.**L.**
Cow. 20/9/43—28/1/44.**G.**
Cow. 27/6—19/7/45.**L.**
Cow. 9/10/46—16/2/47.**G.**
Cow. ?/?—15/3/47.**L.**
Cow. 10/7—22/9/49.**G.**
Cow. 27/9—10/11/51.**L/I.**
Cow. 21/12/51—1/4/52.**C/L.**
Cow. 6—9/4/52.**N/C.**
Cow. 22/5—16/7/54.**G.**
Cow. 1/9—13/10/55.**N/C.**

BOILERS:
7460.
7255 *(ex1644)* 28/11/25.
7611 *(ex4690)* 13/3/28.

7462 *(ex4672)* 19/4/30.
7687 *(ex4665)* 25/11/33.
7686 *(ex4649)* 31/5/41.
8860 *(ex4639)* 28/1/44.
7622 *(ex1736)* 16/2/47.
9199 *(ex1736)* 22/9/49.
9199 reno. 21162 10/11/51.
21153 *(ex61728)* 16/7/54.

SHEDS:
King's Cross.
Stratford 22/2/28.
March 28/11/41.
Colchester 12/1/46.
Stratford 7/12/46.
Colchester 28/12/46.
Stratford 25/9/47.
Colwick 5/10/52.
Darnall 26/6/55.
Lincoln 17/6/56.
Boston 29/12/57.
New England 5/4/59.

RENUMBERED:
4669 13/3/25.
1759 24/8/46.
61759 10/7/49.

CONDEMNED: 1/1/60.
Into Str. for cut up 1/60.

4670

N.B.L. Co. 21981.

To traffic 6/1918.

REPAIRS:
Don. 7/7—30/9/22.**G.**
Don. 17/9—27/12/24.**G.**
Don. 15/4—2/10/26.**G.**
Don. 15/8—1/11/27.**G.**
Don. 16/3—4/5/29.**G.**
Don. 18/10—22/11/30.**G.**
Don. 3/9—15/10/32.**G.**
Don. 27/10—1/12/34.**G.**
Don. 27/2—20/3/37.**G.**
Don. 22/7—26/8/39.**G.**
Don. 27/6—1/8/42.**G.**
Cow. 23/5—1/7/44.**G.**
Cow. 14/1—24/2/45.**L.**
Cow. 15/11/45—12/1/46.**G.**
Cow. 27/9—28/12/46.**G.**
Cow. 12/2—28/3/47.**L.**
Cow. 19/2—21/4/50.**G.**
Cow. 30/4—4/5/50.**N/C.**
Cow. 29/9—25/10/52.**H/I.**
Cow. 12/7—4/9/54.**G.**
Cow. 11/2—20/4/57.**H/I.**

BOILERS:
7461.
7259 *(ex1648)* 30/9/22.
7265 *(ex1656)* 27/12/24.
7262 *(ex4677)* 1/11/27.

The last of the original pattern was the left hand cylinder on 61734 until it went to works on 12th September 1952.

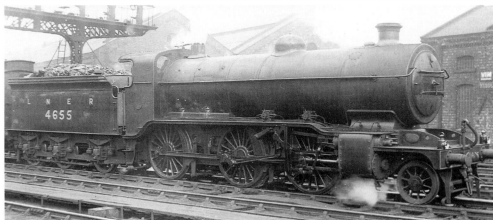

Engines built up to No.4679 were all fitted with piston tail rods which they retained until after 1925. The Kitson built engines did not have them fitted and, as an experiment, the tail rods were removed from three of the earlier engines: 4659 (14/2/25), 4655 (14/3/25) and 4651 (28/3/25). This proved satisfactory and from late 1926 they were gradually taken off all the others. All had gone by the time the number was moved from tender to cab.

Lubrication on Nos.4630 to 4659 was by two mechanical type on the right hand running plate, one for the axleboxes and the other for cylinders and valves.

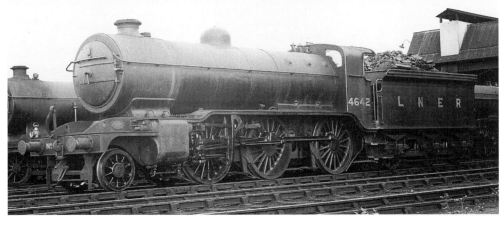

On the left side was only an oil box with two feeds to service the operating rods for the sanding.

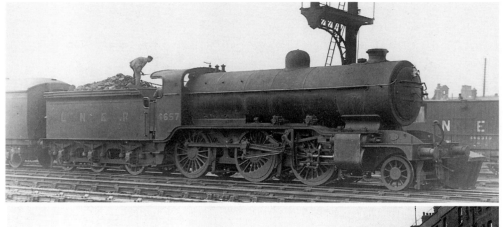

Although No.4657 had two mechanical lubricators as on 4656 seen on the previous page, the feeds to cylinders and motion were quite different in their arrangement, being directly above each valve head.

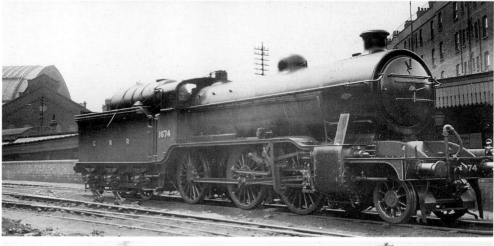

Nos.1660 to 1704 had Detroit sight feed lubricators in the cab with pipes to the cylinders along both sides of the boiler, on Nos.1660 to 1679. The 1921 batch, Nos.1680 to 1704 had the cylinder lubricating pipes only on the left hand side of the boiler, enclosed in a rectangular cover. On the right side there was only the single mechanical lubricator for the axleboxes.

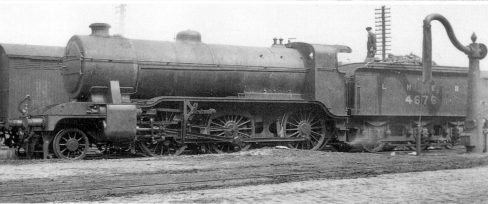

The pipes from the cab sloped slightly downward and, along the boiler side in the small rectangular cover.

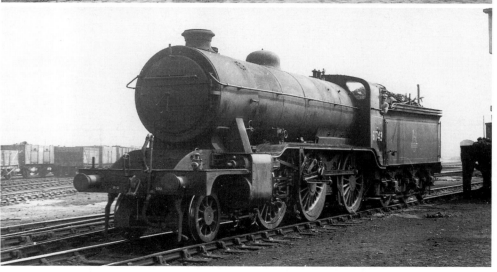

Ex works 27th November 1937, No.4650 had an extra Wakefield mechanical lubricator, on the left hand running plate, to feed the piston valves separately and enabling different oils to be compared. It was the first K2 to be fitted with anti-carboniser. The extra lubricator was also put on No.4653 (11/12/37) and 4641 (29/1/38). As Nos.61731, 61740 and 61743 they kept the extra lubricator to withdrawal.

Ex works 1st October 1921, No.1644 had lost the mechanical lubricator for the cylinders; this had been replaced by a sight-feed lubricator from the SE&CR which had feeds along both sides of the boiler and then through the saddle to the inside steam pipes. Despite changes of boiler in July 1924 and, as here, in January 1929 the lubrication arrangement was not altered. This one-off cylinder lubrication system was changed, probably ex works 4th May 1935, when a new right hand cylinder was put on. It reverted to Wakefield mechanical but of a later type compared with the original still serving the axleboxes.

Nos.4660 to 4679 became 61750 to 61769 and some had late change to their lubrication. Until May 1954 No.61759 kept the original arrangement of feed pipes to the cylinders down both sides of the boiler. Ex works 16th July 1954 it had been changed to the later arrangement of cylinder feed pipe only on the left hand side. Nos.61761, 61763, 61764, 61766, 61767, 61768 and 61769 are known to have had this alteration, No.1768 as early as 17th October 1947.

Most of the class changed their top lamp iron to the Group Standard pattern but No.61745 at 30th August 1959 still had original GNR clover leaf style bracket, so probably retained it to withdrawal on 25th November 1960.

Until after they became LNER, the cross rail on the smokebox door was above the top hinge strap and the boiler side handrails continued round the front edge of the smokebox in an upward curve.

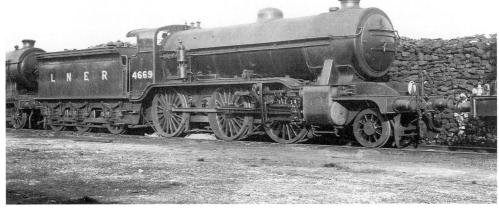

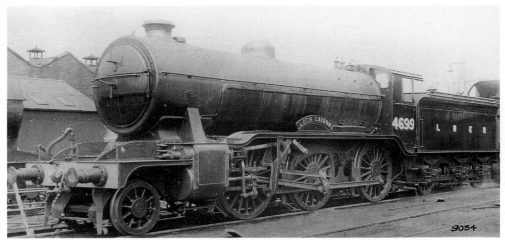

From about 1935, a few had the side rails cut to end on the smokebox but only eight were so observed and at these dates: 4639 (10/3/37), 4681 (1/5/37), 4698 (12/6/36), 4699 (15/9/36), 61736 (30/11/50), 61737 (15/10/50 & 30/3/54), 61748 (30/4/48) and 61779 (2/6/51 & 19/4/54). In addition No.E1773 had the left hand rail cut but the right hand rail was unaltered. Note 4699 had cross rail below top strap and had been changed to Group Standard top lamp iron. Ends of straps now provided door stops. After its 29th June 1946 shopping, a single door stop between the hinge sufficed.

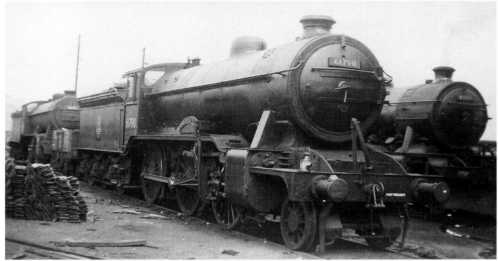

By Nationalisation the standard position for the cross rail was just above the top strap and by moving the Group Standard lamp iron a little higher there was room for the smokebox number plate between them. Most of the class conformed to this arrangement. Note GNR style twin lampirons are still fitted, thirty years after they ceased usage.

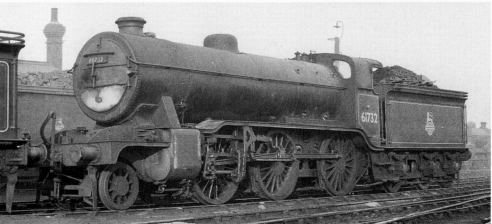

There were few deviations from standard style but No.61732 from March 1952 to at least June 1954 had a short cross rail above the number plate and retained GNR lamp iron in original position. No.61759 ex works 16th July 1954, had this style but with G.S. lamp iron.

Five have been checked as in this style with cross rail below the upper strap: 61737 (15/10/50 & 30/3/54), 61745 (30/8/59), 61752 (9/9/50), 61774 (14/8/54) and 61787 (5/6/51). However, three of these also had standard style whilst in BR livery.

7459 (ex4651) 22/11/30.
8982 (new) 20/3/37.
9194 (new) 26/8/39.
8756 (ex4679) 1/7/44.
C1826 (ex4694) 12/1/46.
9150 (ex1721) 28/12/46.
9150 reno. 21151 25/10/52.
21107 (ex61770) 4/9/54.

SHEDS:
Doncaster.
Brunswick 16/3/25.
Cambridge 13/6/27.
Doncaster 27/7/27.
March 20/6/31.
Doncaster 10/9/31.
Boston 28/6/33.
Doncaster 31/8/33.
March 2/7/35.
Bradford 22/1/36.
Ardsley 25/1/40.
New England 23/2/40.
March 21/5/43.
New England 3/7/43.
Boston 16/6/46.
Darnall 10/7/55.

RENUMBERED:
4670 27/12/24.
1760 7/12/46.
61760 21/4/50.

CONDEMNED: 13/12/60.
Into Don. for cut up 13/12/60.

4671

N.B.L. Co. 21982.

To traffic 6/1918.

REPAIRS:
Don. 2—5/11/21.**L**.
Don. 6/6—29/9/23.**G**.
As *1671*N.
Don. 29/6—10/10/25.**G**.
Don. 15/10/27—5/1/28.**G**.
Don. 3—16/4/28.**L**.
Altered to G.E. gauge.
Westinghouse brake fitted.
Don. 13/12/30—10/1/31.**G**.
Don. 24/9—22/10/32.**G**.
Don. 24/11/34—5/1/35.**G**.
Don. 26/1—9/2/35.**L**.
Don. 28/3—2/5/36.**G**.
Don. 27/11—4/12/37.**G**.
Don. 15/6—13/7/40.**G**.
Don. 2/11/40—3/1/41.**H**.
Don. 7/8—4/9/43.**G**.
Cow. 15/7—1/9/45.**G**.
Str. 29/1—9/2/46.**L**.
Cow. 28/12/48—11/3/49.**G**.
Cow. 20/11/51—26/1/52.**L/I**.
Cow. 28/2—17/4/54.**G**.
Cow. 21/5—3/6/54.**N/C**.

Cow. 24/6—20/8/54.**C/L**.
Cow. 27/10—27/11/54.**C/H**.
Cow. 13/8—6/9/58.**G**.
Don. 8/1/61. *Not repaired.*

BOILERS:
7462.
7260 (ex1649) 10/10/25.
7456 (ex4665) 5/1/28.
7683 (ex4647) 10/1/31.
7607 (ex4657) 22/10/32.
8824 (new) 5/1/35.
9200 (new) 13/7/40.
9197 (ex4656) 1/9/45.
9473 (ex1765) 11/3/49.
9473 reno. 21174 26/1/52.
21141 (ex61727) 17/4/54.
21159 (ex61793) 6/9/58.

SHEDS:
King's Cross.
Doncaster 4/11/25.
Cambridge 23/5/28.
March 4/6/28.
Yarmouth 24/9/29.
March 20/12/29.
Cambridge 21/10/36.
Norwich 1/10/38.
March 18/2/45.
Colchester 13/1/46.
Stratford 25/9/47.
Colchester 1/2/48.
Stratford 16/5/48.
Lincoln 5/10/52.
Boston 13/2/55.
Darnall 10/7/55.
King's Cross 8/1/61.

RENUMBERED:
4671 10/10/25.
1761 2/6/46.
61761 11/3/49.

CONDEMNED: 19/1/61.
Into Don. for cut up 19/1/61.

4672

N.B.L. Co. 21983.

To traffic 6/1918.

REPAIRS:
Don. 28/5—6/10/23.**G**.
Don. 12—17/11/23.**L**.
Don. 2/11/25—3/3/26.**G**.
Don. 10—26/3/26.**L**.
Don. 27/1—13/4/28.**G**.
Altered to G.E. gauge.
Don. 21/12/29—18/1/30.**G**.
Don. 7/5—11/6/32.**G**.
Don. 3/3—7/4/34.**G**.
Don. 21/9—19/10/35.**G**.
Don. 25/9—16/10/37.**G**.
Don. 29/10—8/11/37.**N/C**.

Don. 25/11/39—6/1/40.**G**.
Don. 21/3—25/4/42.**G**.
Cow. 25/4—10/6/44.**G**.
Cow. 10/1—16/2/46.**G**.
Cow. 5/10—18/12/47.**G**.
Cow. 20/6—3/7/48.**L**.
Cow. 15/3—7/5/49.**H/I**.
Cow. 13/5—15/9/51.**G**.
Cow. 4/7—27/8/55.**G**.
Cow. 12—17/9/55.**N/C**.

BOILERS:
7463.
7462 (ex1671) 3/3/26.
7259 (ex4642) 18/1/30.
7838 (ex4667) 19/10/35.
7839 (ex4664) 16/10/37.
8868 (ex4643) 18/12/47.
8868 reno. 21134 15/9/51.
21165 (ex61753) 27/8/55.

SHEDS:
Doncaster.
Ardsley ?/?
Doncaster 1/8/27.
New England 6/8/32.
Boston 26/6/39.
New England 30/9/39.
March 24/5/43.
New England 3/7/43.
Boston 9/6/46.

RENUMBERED:
4672 3/3/26.
1762 28/3/46.
61762 3/7/48.

CONDEMNED: 22/6/59.
Sold for scrap to Motherwell
Machinery & Scrap, Wishaw,
30/11/59.

4673

N.B.L. Co. 21984.

To traffic 6/1918.

REPAIRS:
Don. 1/5—7/10/22.**G**.
Don. 25/7—5/12/24.**G**.
Don. 23/9—26/12/26.**G**.
Franklin grease lubrication to
axles fitted.
Don. 9—19/2/27.**L**.
Don. 13—23/4/27.**L**.
Don. 13/8—12/10/28.**G**.
Altered to G.E. gauge.
Franklin lubrication off.
Don. 26/4—31/5/30.**G**.
Don. 21/11—26/12/31.**G**.
Don. 10/2—17/3/34.**G**.
Don. 14/3—11/4/36.**G**.
Don. 12—26/2/38.**G**.
Don. 16/9—28/10/39.**G**.

Don. 31/8—19/10/40.**G**.
Don. 13/6—18/7/42.**G**.
Cow. 23/3—6/5/44.**G**.
Cow. 6/7—3/8/46.**G**.
Cow. 15/11/48—22/1/49.**G**.
Cow. 25/9—11/11/50.**H/I**.
Cow. 28/4—25/5/51.**N/C**.
Cow. 17/3—16/5/52.**G**.
Cow. 22/5—20/6/53.**C/L**.
Gor. 17/2—8/4/54.**C/L**.
Cow. 1/1—19/2/55.**G**.
Cow. 9/12/57—25/1/58.**G**.

BOILERS:
7464.
7269 (ex1658) 7/10/22.
7625 (ex1704) 5/12/24.
7942 (new) 26/12/26.
7604 (ex4683) 31/5/30.
8866 (new) 11/4/36.
8868 (ex4641) 26/2/38.
9152 (ex4660) 6/5/44.
9192 (ex4662) 3/8/46.
8823 (ex1777) 22/1/49.
21125 (ex61744) 16/5/52.
21176 (ex61783) 19/2/55.
21164 (ex61735) 25/1/58.

SHEDS:
Doncaster.
Frodingham 4/7/43.
Doncaster 25/7/43.
Colwick 23/8/46.
Boston 9/11/58.
Immingham 1/3/59.
New England 15/11/59.

RENUMBERED:
4673 5/12/24.
1763 13/4/46.
61763 22/1/49.

CONDEMNED: 6/2/61.
Into Don. for cut up 6/2/61.

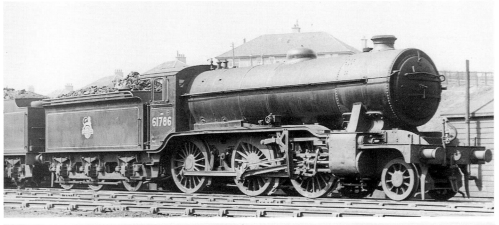

Doncaster did not start taking off the long redundant front lamp iron until during 1931 so the fourteen which went to Scotland in 1924/5 still had it on and Cowlairs took no notice of it until the mid 1950's. The other six which went in 1931/2 included three, Nos.4682, 4685 and 4689, from which Doncaster had removed the surplus iron but Nos.4674, 4684 and 4686 still had it.

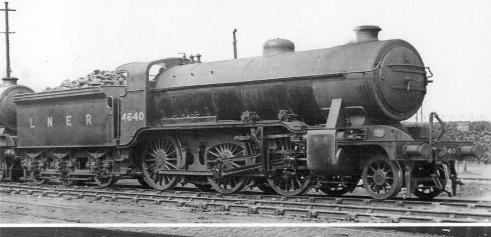

Doncaster continued to repair Southern Area engines until 1946 and from 1931 usually removed the redundant lamp iron, No.4640 losing it 29th April 1933 when ex works.

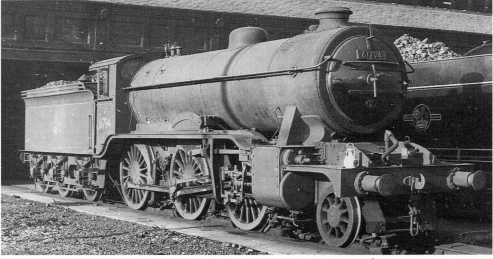

It is doubtful if Cowlairs did remove any surplus lamp irons and No.61794 was still so fitted in this 30th August 1959 photograph. Its final works visit was in September 1958 and it was withdrawn 29th July 1960. From 1953 Doncaster had decided the long guard irons attached to the frame ends were not needed, those on the pony trucks being adequate. By 1954 Cowlairs were taking them off K2 class, No.61786, ex works 10th April 1954 being the first so noted.

The twin lamp irons were also fitted at the tender end to cater for running in reverse, and on the Scottish based engines these also survived.

4674

N.B.L. Co. 21985.

To traffic 7/1918.

LOCH ARKAIG 3/33.

REPAIRS:
Don. 15/10—5/11/21.**L**.
Don. 31/8—8/12/23.**G**.
New chimney to G.E. gauge.
Don. 21/12/25—13/3/26.**G**.
Don. 16—27/3/26.**L**.
Str. ?/?—?/11/27.**L**.
Westinghouse brake fitted.
Don. 17/9—3/11/28.**G**.
Don. 17/10—21/11/31.**G**.
Westinghouse brake removed.
Cow. ?/?—7/4/32.**G**.
Cow. ?/?—3/5/34.**G**.
*Speed indicator off, cab altered
& drop grate fitted.*
Cow. ?/?—21/12/35.**G**.
Cow. 26/6—10/8/37.**G**.
Cow. ?/?—26/1/39.**G**.
Cow. ?/?—1/5/39.**L**.
Cow. ?/?—6/7/40.**G**.
Cow. 28/2—28/3/42.**G**.
Cow. ?/?—28/8/43.**G**.
Cow. ?/?—20/4/45.**L**.
Cow. 8/4—18/5/46.**G**.
Cow. ?/?—17/10/46.**L**.
Cow. ?/?—2/7/47.**H/I**.
Cow. 28/9—20/11/47.**N/C**.
Cow. ?/?—8/1/49.**L/I**.
Cow. ?/?—?/1/50.**N/C**.
Cow. 1/5—24/6/50.**G**.
Cow. ?/?—?/10/50.**N/C**.
Cow. 24/9—18/10/52.**H/I**.
Cow. 6/5—26/6/54.**L/I**.
Cow. 8—15/7/54.**N/C**.
Cow. 19—21/8/54.**N/C**.
Cow. 19—21/9/55.**N/C**.
Cow. 19/3—5/5/56.**G**.
Cow. 24/4—24/5/58.**H/I**.

BOILERS:
7465.
7263 *(ex1651)* 13/3/26.
7549 *(ex4658)* 3/11/28.
7606 *(ex4650)* 21/11/31.
7606 reno.C1788 7/4/32.
8842 *(ex4697)* 28/3/42.
9194 *(ex4641)* 18/5/46.
8559 *(ex61757)* 24/6/50.
8559 reno. 21109 18/10/52.
21145 *(ex61784)* 5/5/56.

SHEDS:
King's Cross.
Stratford *by* 3/24.
Cambridge 4/1/27.
Stratford 3/11/28.
Southend 15/3/30.

Stratford 22/3/30.
Eastfield 11/12/31.
St Margarets ?/8/38.
Eastfield ?/12/42.

RENUMBERED:
4674 13/3/26.
1764 2/6/46.
61764 8/1/49.

CONDEMNED: 7/9/61.
Into Cow. for cut up 1/12/61.

4675

N.B.L. Co. 21986.

To traffic 7/1918.

REPAIRS:
Don. 10/8—30/10/20.**G**.
Don. 10/4—18/7/22.**G**.
Don. 16/1—10/2/23.**L**.
Don. 26/6—15/11/24.**G**.
Don. 5—28/11/25.**L**.
Don. 17/1—30/4/27.**G**.
Westinghouse pump fitted..
Don. 8/8—3/9/27.**L**.
Westinghouse brake completed.
Don. 25/1—22/2/30.**G**.
Don. 16/1—27/2/32.**G**.
Don. 2/6—14/7/34.**G**.
Don. 27/2—20/3/37.**G**.
Don. 23/9—4/11/39.**G**.
Don. 3/1—7/2/42.**G**.
Cow. 9/5—17/6/44.**G**.
Cow. 2/1—14/2/45.**L**.
Don. 30/3—18/5/46.**G**.
Cow. 6/12/48—19/2/49.**G**.
Cow. 1/9—12/10/50.**H/I**.
Str. 26/10—17/11/51.**C/L**.
Cow. 20/6—16/8/52.**G**.
Cow. 11/8—24/9/55.**L/I**.

BOILERS:
7466.
7687 *(new)* 15/11/24.
7454 *(ex4663)* 22/2/30.
7685 *(ex4645)* 14/7/34.
7840 *(ex4646)* 4/11/39.
9473 *(new)* 18/5/46.
9192 *(ex1763)* 19/2/49.
21178 *(new)* 16/8/52.

SHEDS:
Ardsley.
Doncaster ?/?
Stratford 2/9/27.
March 23/2/40.
Colchester 13/1/46.
Stratford 25/9/47.
Lincoln 5/10/52.
Boston 10/7/55.

RENUMBERED:
4675 15/11/24.
1765 27/5/46.
61765 19/2/49.

CONDEMNED: 1/5/58.

4676

N.B.L. Co. 21987.

To traffic 8/1918.

REPAIRS:
Don. 2/10—18/11/22.**L**.
Don. 12/3—1/11/23.**G**.
Don. 12/6—26/9/25.**G**.
Don. 6/3—10/4/26.**L**.
Don. 11/12/26—21/5/27.**G**.
Altered to G.E. gauge.
Don. 8—15/10/27.**L**.
Westinghouse brake fitted.
Don. 11/5—15/6/29.**G**.
H.A. at front fitted.
Don. 21/2—21/3/31.**G**.
Don. 20/1—24/2/34.**G**.
Don. 21/9—19/10/35.**G**.
Don. 10—24/4/37.**G**.
Don. 13/5—17/6/39.**G**.
Don. 13/9—18/10/41.**G**.
Don. 29/11—27/12/41.**L**.
Str. 1/3—7/4/44.**G**.
Cow. 22/11—23/12/44.**L**.
Cow. 22/3—31/5/46.**G**.
Don. 30/1—18/2/48.**L**.
Cow. 15/5—13/8/49.**G**.
Cow. 29/4/50.**N/C**.
Cow. 17/11/52—17/1/53.**L/I**.
Str. 17—26/9/53.**C/L**.
Cow. 20/10—27/11/54.**G**.
Westinghouse brake removed.
Cow. 4—30/8/58.**G**.

BOILERS:
7467.
7466 *(ex1675)* 26/9/25.
7465 *(ex4655)* 15/6/29.
8560 *(new)* 24/2/34.
9008 *(new)* 24/4/37.
7837 *(ex4665)* 17/6/39.
9347 *(new)* 7/4/44.
8561 *(ex4651)* 31/5/46.
8561 reno. 21111 17/1/53.
21169 *(ex61781)* 27/11/54.
21136 *(ex61790)* 30/8/58.

SHEDS:
Ardsley.
March ?/24.
Cambridge ?/?
King's Cross 15/8/25.
Doncaster 23/10/25.
Cambridge 15/10/27.
Stratford 7/1/28.
Doncaster 14/6/29.

Lowestoft 17/9/29.
Doncaster 31/12/29.
March 21/6/31.
Doncaster 9/9/31.
Yarmouth 3/10/31.
Norwich 26/3/33.
Yarmouth 9/10/34.
Lowestoft 3/11/34.
Norwich 28/12/34.
Yarmouth 4/10/36.
Norwich 24/1/37.
March 24/2/40.
Colchester 12/1/46.
South Lynn 4/4/48.
Boston 29/6/52.
Thornton Jct 25/1/53.
Boston 25/3/53.
Immingham 1/3/59.
Colwick 12/6/60.

RENUMBERED:
4676 26/9/25.
1766 16/11/46.
E1766 18/2/48.
61766 13/8/49.

CONDEMNED: 23/1/61.
Into Don. for cut up 25/1/61.

4677

N.B.L. Co. 21988.

To traffic 8/1918.

REPAIRS:
Don. 18/9—30/12/22.**G**.
Don. 26/6—25/10/24.**G**.
Don. 20/5—15/9/26.**G**.
Don. 22/9—25/10/26.**L**.
Don. 16/6—24/9/27.**G**.
Don. 20/7—24/8/29.**G**.
Don. 8/2—8/3/30.**G**.
Don. 10/10—7/11/31.**G**.
*Westinghouse brake fitted
ex4674.*
Don. 9/9—28/10/33.**G**.
Don. 1—22/2/36.**G**.
Str. 29/5—8/6/37.**L**.
Don. 30/4—21/5/38.**G**.
Don. 2/3—6/4/40.**G**.
Don. 1/11/41—7/2/42.**G**.
Cow. 26/3—5/5/44.**G**.
Don. 16/3—13/4/46.**G**.
Cow. 14/5—29/6/46.**L**.
Cow. 6/5—12/6/48.**G**.
Cow. 25/7—7/10/48.**L**.
Str. 28/4—20/5/49.**C/L**.
Cow. 2/8—30/9/50.**L/I**.
Cow. 1—28/3/53.**G**.
Cow. 27/8—1/10/55.**H/I**.
Cow. 25/8—21/9/56.**N/C**.
Cow. 16/4—10/5/58.**G**.

On the original set of smokeboxes there was no provision for any door stop to prevent the door swinging too far.

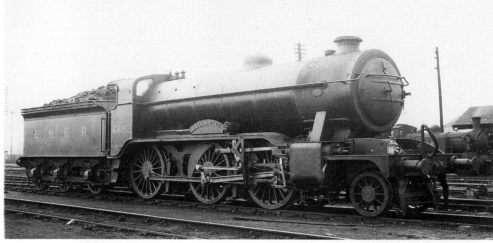

By 1933, where an original door was still in use, a stop was fitted between the hinges on the front rim of the smokebox. This single stop was still to be seen on No.61787 at 28th March 1959.

Where new smokebox doors had to be fitted, as on No.4698 in January 1937, the straps were extended at the hinges and shaped to provide an effective stop.

All were fitted with parallel shank buffers with hollow spindle and circular flange. Only one had a change of buffer type, the rest remained unchanged to withdrawal.

(right) On 28th October 1931, No.4702 went into Gateshead works having been in collision at Blaydon with C7 class No.2203. It was out on the 6th November fitted with Group Standard buffers but not G.S. drawhook, and remained the only one so equipped.

(below) The engines working the West Highland line were made suitable for carrying a small snow plough from 1933. The vacuum standpipe was moved behind the buffer beam, its height was cut, and fixing bolts were provided on the running plate. Pads were put between buffer flanges and beam. Note the standpipe is still carrying the GN load class collar showing E1.

YEADON'S REGISTER

BOILERS:
7468.
7262 (ex1657) 30/12/22.
7460 (ex4669) 15/9/26.
7625 (ex4659) 24/8/29.
8865 (new) 22/2/36.
9346 (ex4655) 5/5/44.
C1788 (ex1790) 12/6/48.
21148 (ex61779) 28/3/53.
21172 (ex61794) 10/5/58.

SHEDS:
Doncaster.
Stratford 14/12/31.
March 5/2/42.
Stratford 13/1/46.
Parkeston 9/2/46.
Stratford 25/9/47.
Lincoln 5/10/52.
Boston 27/6/54.
Immingham 1/3/59.
Colwick 12/6/60.

RENUMBERED:
4677 25/10/24.
1767 13/10/46.
61767 12/6/48.

CONDEMNED: 6/1/61.
Into Don. for cut up 6/1/61.

4678

N.B.L. Co. 21989.

To traffic 8/1918.

REPAIRS:
Don. 5/12/22—1/7/23.**G.**
Don. 19/3—20/6/25.**G.**
Don. 21/11/25—23/1/26.**L.**
Don. 27/1—20/6/28.**G.**
Don. 12/4—17/5/30.**G.**
Don. 14/11—26/12/31.**G.**
Don. 29/7—2/9/33.**G.**
Don. 13/4—11/5/35.**G.**
Don. 5—26/2/38.**G.**
Don. 20/7—24/8/40.**G.**
Don. 16/1—20/2/43.**G.**
Cow. 15/8—7/10/44.**G.**
Cow. 31/3—24/10/47.**G.**
Don. 28/7—21/8/48.**L.**
Cow. 11/4—3/6/50.**G.**
Cow. 27/11—9/12/50.**C/L.**
Cow. 31/7—6/9/52.**G.**
Cow. 13/9—4/11/54.**G.**
Cow. 25/11—7/12/54.**N/C.**
Cow. 5/5—29/6/57.**H/I.**
Cow. 26/9—19/10/57.**N/C.**
Dar. 22/1/59. Not repaired.

BOILERS:
7469.
7468 (ex1677) 1/7/23.
7300 (ex4659) 20/6/28.

7942 (ex4683) 2/9/33.
9076 (new) 26/2/38.
8861 (ex4658) 20/2/43.
8843 (ex4652) 24/10/47.
9193 (ex61738) 3/6/50.
21116 (ex61763) 6/9/52.
21167 (ex61739) 4/11/54.

SHEDS:
Doncaster.
York 11/8/25.
Doncaster 1/4/26.
Norwich 25/7/35.
Yarmouth 5/10/35.
Norwich 17/12/35.
Ardsley 30/1/36.
Bradford 5/5/37.
Ardsley 27/10/37.
Bradford 9/5/38.
Ardsley 25/1/40.
New England 23/2/40.
Doncaster 3/4/42.
Ardsley 30/7/45.
Colwick 18/8/46.

RENUMBERED:
4678 20/6/25.
1768 17/11/46.
61768 21/8/48.

CONDEMNED: 26/1/59.
Cut up at Darlington.

4679

N.B.L. Co. 21990.

To traffic 8/1918.

REPAIRS:
Don. 31/5—11/6/21.**L.**
Don. 15/8—3/11/23.**G.**
Don. 4/8—14/11/25.**G.**
Don. 26/1—1/6/28.**G.**
Don. 18/1—15/2/30.**G.**
Don. 31/10—5/12/31.**G.**
Don. 30/9—28/10/33.**G.**
Don. 2/6—14/7/34.**G.**
Don. 23/5—27/6/36.**G.**
Don. 25/3—29/4/39.**G.**
Don. 30/8—4/10/41.**G.**
Cow. ?/?—25/3/44.**G.**
Str. ?/?—19/5/45.**L.**
Str. 17—29/9/45.**L.**
Cow. 16/5—15/6/46.**G.**
Cow. ?/?—15/5/47.**L.**
Cow. 30/8—23/10/48.**H/I.**
Cow. 20/2—19/5/51.**G.**
Side window cab fitted.
Cow. 1—6/6/51.**N/C.**
Cow. 5—17/5/52.**C/L.**
Cow. 27/4—23/5/53.**L/I.**
Cow. 11/3—30/4/55.**G.**
Cow. 25—28/1/56.**N/C.**
Cow. 11/12/57—11/1/58.**H/I.**

BOILERS:
7470.
7455 (ex1664) 14/11/25.
7253 (ex4641) 1/6/28.
7686 (ex4666) 28/10/33.
8756 (new) 14/7/34.
8978 (ex4634) 25/3/44.
21171 (ex61741) 19/5/51.
21137 (ex61722) 30/4/55.

SHEDS:
King's Cross.
New England 29/2/40.
Doncaster 4/4/42.
Bradford 30/7/45.
Ardsley 2/12/45.
Colwick 18/8/46.
Eastfield 20/5/51.
Parkhead 24/2/52.

RENUMBERED:
4679 3/3/25.
1769 1/11/46.
61769 23/10/48.

CONDEMNED: 2/9/60.
Into Cow. for cut up 12/11/60.

4680

Kitson 5330.

To traffic 6/1921.

REPAIRS:
Don. 5/12/23—22/3/24.**G.**
Don. 27/3—4/4/24.**L.**
Don. 8/2—27/3/26.**L.**
Don. 16/6—16/10/26.**G.**
Don. 30/10—12/12/28.**G.**
Don. 6/12/30—17/1/31.**G.**
Don. 12/12/31—9/1/32.**G.**
Don. 2/9—14/10/33.**G.**
Don. 27/7—31/8/35.**G.**
Don. 14—29/8/36.**L.**
Don. 19/6—24/7/37.**G.**
Don. 10/12/38—7/1/39.**G.**
Don. 18/11/39—16/1/40.**G.**
Don. 29/11/41—10/1/42.**G.**
Don. 6—27/11/43.**G.**
Cow. 25/12/44—25/1/45.**C/H.**
Cow. 18/5—12/7/45.**L.**
Cow. 6/6—13/7/46.**G.**
Cow. 6/8—6/11/48.**G.**
Cow. 26/11/50—13/1/51.**H/I.**
Cow. 2/6—8/7/52.**H/I.**
Cow. 21/4—22/5/54.**G.**
Cow. 1—8/6/54.**N/C.**
Cow. 1/8—8/9/56.**L/I.**

BOILERS:
7601.
7258 (ex4668) 12/12/28.
7261 (ex4653) 17/1/31.
9010 (new) 24/7/37.

7546 (ex4666) 10/1/42.
8866 (ex4634) 27/11/43.
9076 (ex4642) 25/1/45.
8842 (ex4674) 13/7/46.
C1828 (ex1756) 6/11/48.
21132 (ex61749) 22/5/54.

SHEDS:
New England.
King's Cross 1/10/31.
Colwick 7/9/36.
Boston 8/1/50.
Eastfield 14/1/51.
Thornton Jct 1/1/52.
Dunfermline 28/9/52.

RENUMBERED:
4680 22/3/24.
1770 13/7/46.
61770 6/11/48.

CONDEMNED: 8/7/59.
Sold for scrap to J.N.Connell,
Coatbridge, 28/10/59.

4681

Kitson 5331.

To traffic 6/1921.

REPAIRS:
Don. 22/11/23—5/4/24.**G.**
Don. 27/2—15/6/26.**G.**
Don. 14/3—28/7/28.**G.**
Altered to G.E. gauge.
Don. 6/9—18/10/30.**G.**
Don. 12/12/31—9/1/32.**G.**
Don. 15/7—2/9/33.**G.**
Don. 13/4—11/5/35.**G.**
Don. 12/12/36—9/1/37.**G.**
Don. 15—22/12/37.**N/C.**
Don. 22/4—27/5/39.**G.**
Don. 29/3—26/4/41.**G.**
Cow. 7—26/10/43.**G.**
Cow. 8/1—9/3/46.**G.**
Don. 12/1—29/4/48.**G.**
Cow. 2/7—2/9/50.**G.**
Cow. 18/8—24/9/52.**G.**
Cow. 11/1—27/2/54.**G.**
Cow. 11/12/56—2/2/57.**G.**
Cow. 24—31/10/57.**C/L.**

BOILERS:
7602.
7608 (ex4687) 28/7/28.
8827 (new) 11/5/35.
8864 (ex spare) 9/3/46.
9076 (ex 4680) 29/4/48.
9076 reno. 21150 24/9/52.
21123 (ex61772) 27/2/54.
21127 (ex61755) 2/2/57.

SHEDS:
New England.

It soon became usual to leave the bracket fixed to the running plate, note drilled holes along the base of the buffer beam, and that No.4698 did not at first have pads behind the flanges. Later, when other Scottish engines were prepared for taking a snow plough, the standpipe remained in front of the bufferbeam and at the same height.

(right) The small snow plough fitted under the buffer beam and was carried by the bracket attached to the running plate.

(below) It was not until BR days that 61786 was fitted for snow plough, and although the standpipe was reduced in height it was left in front of the buffer beam. The middle lamp iron was made taller and of a stepped type not seen on any other K2.

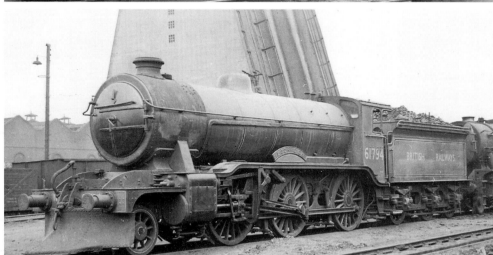

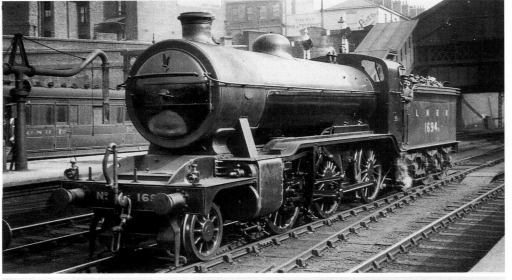

All had this GN design cab with whistle above the roof making it 13ft 4⅝in. above rail level. Apart from those cut down specially to be transferred to the GE and NB sections, from 1927 engines working on the GN Section were also brought within 13ft 1in. gauge. Apart from No.4692 in February 1933, those engines which retained the GN design cab never had hinged glass side screens fitted.

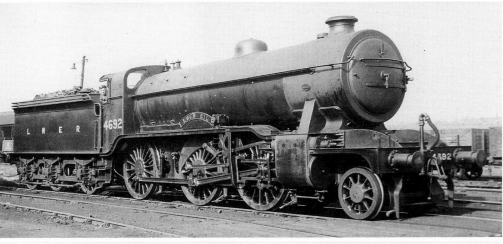

The fourteen transferred to Scottish Area in 1924/5 and the further six in 1931/2, all kept the GN design cab and it was September 1932 before any alteration began. Beginning with No.4692 in February 1933, ten engines were fitted with nameplates before they had any alteration made to their cab. No.4692 was the only one to have side screens fitted and they were removed in July 1934 when a side window cab was put on.

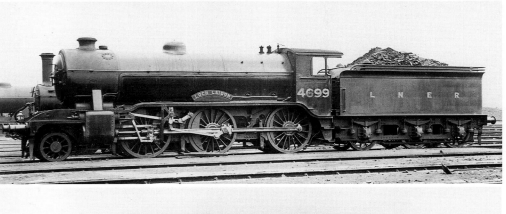

Only two, Nos.4685 in December 1933 and No.4699 in June 1934, were named and got the cab alteration at the same works visit. No.4699 was the last of the thirteen to be named. The seven allocated to Edinburgh St Margarets shed, Nos.4686, 4689, 4694, 4695, 4696, 4702 and 4703, did not get names but were fitted with side window cabs.

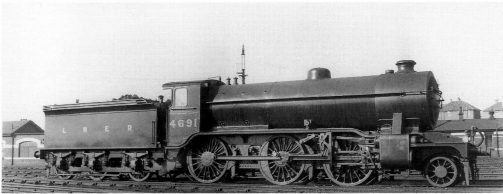

Ex Cowlairs in September 1932, No.4691 had been changed from GN type cab to one with a single side window, but the roof was only extended one inch further back.

King's Cross 3/2/32.
New England 19/3/34.
Boston 3/8/39.
New England 14/5/40.
Boston 15/6/40.
Colwick 16/4/45.
Boston 16/3/58.
Immingham 1/3/59.
Colwick 4/9/60.

RENUMBERED:
4681 5/4/24.
1771 20/10/46.
61771 29/4/48.

CONDEMNED: 16/12/60.
Into Don. for cut up 16/12/60.

4682

Kitson 5332.

To traffic 6/1921.

LOCH LOCHY 22/4/33.

REPAIRS:
Don. 5/12/23—19/4/24.**G.**
Don. 25/3—7/8/26.**G.**
Don. 1/4—11/6/27.**G.**
Don. 5/3—27/7/28.**G.**
Don. 24/5—28/6/30.**G.**
Don. 25/7—29/8/31.**G.**
Don. 5/9—17/10/31.**L.**
Cow. ?/?—?/?/32.**?.**
Cow. ?/?—22/4/33.**G.**
Cow. ?/?—13/7/34.**G.**
Side window cab & drop grate fitted.
Cow. ?/?—12/7/35.**G.**
Cow. ?/?—23/1/37.**G.**
Cow. ?/?—?/11/37.**L.**
Cow. ?/?—20/5/38.**G.**
Cow. ?/?—24/6/38.**L.**
Cow. ?/?—7/7/39.**L.**
Cow. ?/12/39—10/1/40.**G.**
Cow. ?/?—27/3/40.**L.**
Cow. ?/?—7/2/41.**L.**
Cow. ?/?—25/4/42.**G.**
Cow. 23/10—4/12/43.**G.**
Cow. ?/?—13/2/45.**L.**
Cow. 7/5—8/6/46.**G.**
Cow. ?/?—9/5/47.**N/C.**
Cow. 30/1—27/2/48.**G.**
Cow. 31/3—1/4/48.**N/C.**
Cow. 6/6—2/7/49.**L/I.**
Cow. 1/1—2/2/51.**H/I.**
Cow. 1/5—12/6/52.**L/I.**
Cow. 18/11—12/12/53.**G.**
Cow. 26/7—7/8/54.**C/L.**
Cow. 8/11—3/12/55.**H/I.**
Cow. 14—17/12/55.**N/C.**
Cow. 26/8—28/9/57.**G.**

BOILERS:
7603.
7251 *(ex4640)* 27/7/28.
7251 reno. C1785 ?/?/32.
7615 *(ex4694)* 22/4/33.
C1826 *(ex4698)* 23/1/37.
7616 *(ex4700)* 10/1/40.
9072 *(ex4693)* 4/12/43.
8844 *(ex1731)* 27/2/48.
8844 reno. 21123 2/2/51.
21126 *(ex61778)* 12/12/53.
21135 *(ex61788)* 28/9/57.

SHEDS:
New England,
Eastfield 29/10/31.
St Margarets ?/1/39.
Eastfield ?/9/42.
Parkhead 20/11/49.

RENUMBERED:
4682 19/4/24.
1772 25/8/46.
61772 1/4/48.

CONDEMNED: 25/11/59.
Into Cow. for cut up 23/1/60.

4683

Kitson 5333.

To traffic 6/1921.

REPAIRS:
Don. 29/11/23—15/3/24.**G.**
Don. 26/3—9/4/24.**L.**
Don. 15/4—12/8/26.**G.**
Don. 26/8—21/11/28.**G.**
Don. 1/11—6/12/30.**G.**
Don. 5/11—3/12/32.**G.**
Don. 1—29/9/34.**G.**
Don. 30/5—4/7/36.**G.**
Don. 25/9—16/10/37.**G.**
Don. 30/7—20/8/38.**G.**
Don. 2/3—6/4/40.**G.**
Don. 2—30/5/42.**G.**
Cow. 14/7—29/8/44.**G.**
Don. 30/3—18/5/46.**G.**
Don. 6/2—12/3/48.**G.**
Cow. 6/3—24/4/50.**G.**
Cow. 29/7—4/10/52.**G.**
Cow. 10/6—4/7/53.**C/L.**
Gor. 28/4—25/6/54.**N/C.**
Cow. 27/11/54—29/1/55.**G.**
Cow. 27/2—19/4/58.**G.**

BOILERS:
7604.
7470 *(ex4661)* 21/11/28.
7942 *(ex4673)* 6/12/30.
7264 *(ex4687)* 3/12/32.
8759 *(new)* 29/9/34.
9150 *(new)* 20/8/38.
7837 *(ex4676)* 29/8/44.

9474 *(new)* 18/5/46.
21147 *(ex61790)* 4/10/52.
21111 *(ex61766)* 29/1/55.
21187 *(ex61742)* 19/4/58.

SHEDS:
New England.
Stratford 13/10/34.
Colwick 26/10/36.
Boston 9/11/58.
Immingham 1/3/59.
Colwick 4/9/60.

RENUMBERED:
4683 15/3/24.
1773 17/11/46.
E1773 12/3/48.
61773 24/4/50.

CONDEMNED: 23/12/60.
Into Don. for cut up 23/12/60.

4684

Kitson 5334.

To traffic 6/1921.

LOCH GARRY 7/33

REPAIRS:
Don. 28/11/23—19/4/24.**G.**
Don. 15/3—3/7/26.**G.**
Don. 16/11/28—3/1/29.**G.**
Altered to G.E. gauge.
Don. 24/8—28/9/29.**G.**
Don. 3—24/10/31.**G.**
Cow. ?/?—1/1/33.**?.**
Cow. ?/?—2/11/34.**G.**
Side window cab & drop grate fitted.
Cow. ?/3—22/4/36.**G.**
Cow. ?/?—19/8/37.**G.**
Cow. ?/?—13/10/38.**L.**
Cow. ?/?—14/10/39.**G.**
Cow. ?/?—?/11/39.**L.**
Cab screens fitted.
Cow. ?/?—15/8/40.**L.**
Cow. ?/?—30/11/40.**G.**
Hudd A.T.C. fitted.
Cow. ?/?—14/6/41.**C/H.**
Cow. ?/?—3/9/41.**L.**
Cow. ?/?—4/7/42.**L.**
Cow. ?/?—11/7/42.**L.**
Hudd removed.
Cow. ?/?—8/3/43.**H.**
Cow. ?/?—21/12/43.**L.**
Cow. ?/?—10/3/45.**L.**
Cow. 7/9—10/10/45.**G.**
Cow. ?/?—23/11/45.**?.**
Snow plough fitted.
Cow. ?/?—6/4/46.**C/H.**
Cow. 9/4—8/5/47.**H.**
Cow. ?/?—26/6/48.**L.**
Cow. 17/2—20/8/49.**G.**

Cow. 30/1—3/3/51.**L/I.**
Cow. 24/6—18/7/52.**L/I.**
Cow. 10/6—14/8/54.**G.**
Cow. 23/5—9/7/55.**C/L.**
Cow. 7/1—11/2/56.**H/I.**
Cow. 27/8—15/9/56.**C/L.**
Cow. 28/11/56—19/1/57.**N/C.**
Cow. 6—16/3/57.**N/C.**

BOILERS:
7605.
7464 *(ex1673)* 19/4/24.
7838 *(new)* 3/7/26.
7470 *(ex4683)* 24/10/31.
7470 reno. C1786 1/1/33.
C1787 *(ex4685)* 22/4/36.
C1828 *(ex4686)* 30/11/40.
8824 *(ex4671)* 14/6/41.
8562 *(ex4644)* 10/10/45.
9151 *(ex4645)* 6/4/46.
C1827 *(ex1747)* 20/8/49.
C1827 reno. 21106 3/3/51.
21174 *(ex61761)* 14/8/54.

SHEDS:
New England.
Eastfield 17/11/31.
St Margarets ?/2/40.
Eastfield ?/9/42.

RENUMBERED:
4684 19/4/24.
1774 17/11/46.
61774 26/6/48.

CONDEMNED: 16/4/58.
Cut up at Kilmarnock.

4685

Kitson 5335.

To traffic 6/1921.

LOCH TREIG 12/33

REPAIRS:
Don. 21—25/6/21.**L.**
Don. 13—25/11/22.**L.**
Don. 1/5—11/8/23.**G.**
Don. 14/7—10/10/25.**G.**
Don. 4/8—3/11/27.**G.**
Don. 15/6—20/7/29.**G.**
Don. 27/9—25/10/30.**G.**
Don. 11—18/4/31.**L.**
Don. 29/8—17/10/31.**G.**
Cow. ?/?—?/?/32.**?.**
Cow. ?/?—?/12/33.**G.**
Side window cab & drop grate fitted.
Cow. ?/12—?/12/33.**L.**
Cow. ?/?—?/2/34.**L.**
Cow. ?/?—29/10/34.**G.**
Cow. ?/?—5/10/35.**G.**
Cow. ?/?—?/11/35.**L.**

The next to have altered cab was No.4703 in October 1933 and the cab roof had been extended by a further nine inches to give added protection. When No.4694 was altered in February 1935, all twenty of the Scottish area engines then had the side window cab.

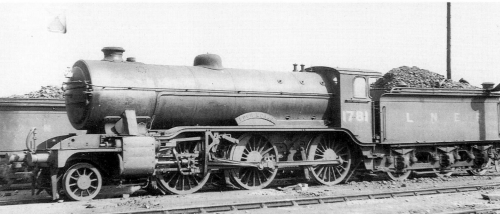

(left) No.4691 (1781 from 5th May 1946) got the longer cab roof at its March 1935 repair. It was reported as having been fitted with cab side screens when ex works 28th December 1940 but as shown here, ex works 12th October 1946, there is no evidence of them.

(below) The altered cab had rain strips on the roof and the window was a sliding type giving the option still of open cab when desired.

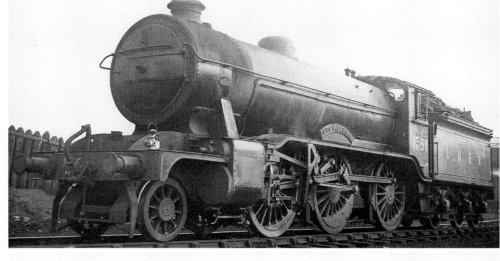

Commencing with No.4689 (*see* photo on page 27), ex works 25th August 1938, hinged glass side screens were gradually added to those which had side window cabs.

When K1 class were rebuilt to K2, the cab had to be set back 5½in. On Nos.1631 and 1635, done before Grouping and on Nos.4630, 4633 and 4634 (altered 1931-33) the cab was shortened so that the rear edge lined up with the end of the frame, which was not altered. On the first three rebuilds, Nos.1631, 1635 and 4634 (6/31) the horizontal rail on the cabside was not lifted to match the higher position of the boiler rails. On Nos.4630 (10/32) and 4633 (1/33) it was lifted. When the other five were rebuilt, Nos.4632, 4636, 4637, 4638 and 4639, from December 1935 to July 1937, they had a 3½in. rear extension made to their frames so that their cabs did not need to be shortened (*see* 4633 on page 18). Their cab rail was also lifted to boiler rail level.

Until after the end of the LNER the cab situation remained as outlined above, but Nos.61721 and 61729 (ex 4631 and 4639) had further cab change. No.4639 (No.1729 from 28th April 1946) was transferred to Scottish Area on 14th December 1945 in exchange for No.3445, and ex Cowlairs 1st October 1949 had been changed to a side window cab. The reverse exchange with the K1/1 took place on 13th November 1949 and 61729 was the only English K2 to have side window cab.

Between 14th January and 3rd June 1951, ten more K2 class, Nos.61721, 61722, 61733, 61734, 61735, 61741, 61755, 61758, 61769 and 61770, went permanently to the Scottish Region. All these duly had change of cab to side window type.

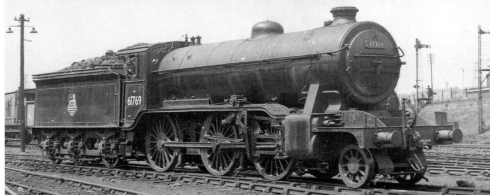

Amongst these late cab alterations, No.61733 and 61755 seem to have been exceptions in not having side screens fitted. Nos.61721, 61735, 61758, 61769 and 61770 certainly had them.

Five - Nos.1738 (12/47 to 4/51), 61740 (10/49 to 1/51), 1742 (11/47 to 10/52), 1743 (11/47 to 11/51) and 1748 (11/47 to 9/53), worked on the Midland & Great Northern system and Whittaker tablet catchers were fitted on their tenders.

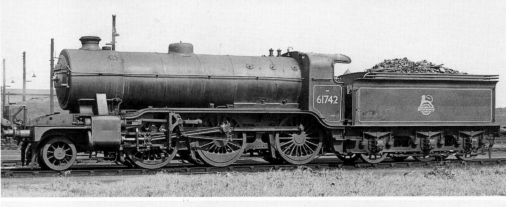

When these engines left the M&GN the tablet apparatus was taken off but evidence of its fitting could still be seen. When 61742 had a general repair at Cowlairs and was out on 9th May 1953, it had one of the ten newly built boilers which could account for the flat topped dome cover.

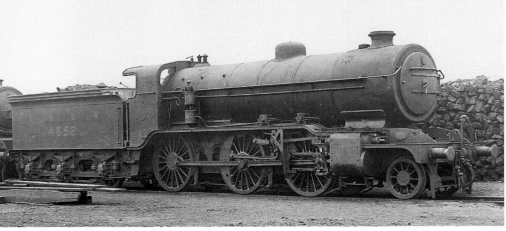

Although carriage heating apparatus was provided, it was not until the late 1920's that a front end connection was added, and then only to those working on the G.E. Section.

The twenty transferred to Scottish Area by the LNER did not have a heater connection at the front end but some of the ten sent to Scottish sheds in 1951 had worked on the GE Section and therefore were so fitted. No.4693, one of the original twenty sent to Scotland, was unusual in only having a 3-link loose coupling when the screw adjustable type was standard.

During the lengthy coal strike in 1921, seven K2's were fitted for burning oil fuel from the cylindrical 1000 gallons tank mounted on the tender. In November 1921 when coal supplies were readily available again, the oil firing equipment was removed. In 1926 when a six months coal strike disrupted supplies again, the K2 class was not among those engines fitted for oil firing.

Ex works 23rd August 1930, No.4647 (later 61737) was fitted with a Stone's smokebox ash ejector and this was still in use at least to July 1953. It was the only K2 so equipped. A 2in. diameter pipe was fitted under the front of the box and this led down between the frames to discharge on the track. The device survived repairs by the works at Doncaster, Stratford and Cowlairs so may still have remained to the November 1956 withdrawal of 61737.

Cow. ?/?—9/11/36.**H.**
Cow. ?/?—?/1/37.**L.**
Cow. 5/2—11/3/38.**G.**
Cow. ?/?—8/6/38.**L.**
Cow. ?/?—?/2/40.**G.**
Cab screens fitted.
Cow. ?/?—15/8/41.**G.**
Hudd A.T.C. fitted.
Cow. ?/?—20/12/41.**L.**
Hudd removed.
Cow. ?/?—2/5/42.**L.**
Cow. ?/?—25/3/43.**L.**
Cow. 19/6—17/7/43.**H.**
Cow. ?/?—7/2/44.**L.**
Cow. ?/?—17/3/45.**G.**
Cow. 6—30/10/46.**G.**
Cow. ?—31/5/47.**N/C.**
Cow. 18/5—2/7/48.**H/I.**
Cow. 1/9—8/10/49.**H/I.**
Cow. 24/8—6/10/51.**G.**
Cow. 20/4—20/5/53.**H/I.**
Cow. 23/2—27/3/54.**C/L.**
Cow. 15/3—14/5/55.**G.**
Cow. 25—28/5/55.**N/C.**
Cow. 5/12/56—4/1/57.**L/I.**

BOILERS:
7606.
7267 *(ex4686)* 3/11/27.
7455 *(ex4679)* 20/7/29.
7455 reno. C1787 ?/?32.
7623 *(ex4699)* 5/10/35.
7613 *(ex4697)* 11/3/38.
C1786 *(ex4700)* 17/7/43.
8827 *(ex4681)* 30/10/46.
21166 *(ex61726)* 6/10/51.
21160 *(ex61776)* 14/5/55.

SHEDS:
Doncaster.
Eastfield 30/10/31.

RENUMBERED:
1685N 11/8/23.
4685 *by* 5/25.
1775 10/2/46.
61775 2/7/48.

CONDEMNED: 2/5/58.
Cut up at Kilmarnock.

4686

Kitson 5336.

To traffic 6/1921.

REPAIRS:
Don. 26—29/4/22.**L.**
Don. 19/1—14/4/23.**G.**
Don. 15/12/24—26/3/25.**G.**
Don. 28/8—15/9/25.**L.**
Don. 29/9—10/10/25.**L.**
Don. 11—15/5/26.**L.**
Don. 14/3—25/6/27.**G.**

Don. 13/3—11/5/28.**L.**
Don. 29/9—24/11/28.**G.**
Don. 31/5—5/7/30.**G.**
Don. 2—7/5/31.**L.**
Don. 5/12/31—9/1/32.**G.**
Cow. ?/?—?/?/32.**?.**
Cow. ?/?—29/11/34.**G.**
Side window cab & drop grate fitted.
Cow. ?/?—2/5/36.**G.**
Cow. ?/?—13/9/37.**G.**
Cow. ?/?—?/10/37.**L.**
Cow. ?/?—26/10/38.**G.**
Cow. ?/?—13/7/40.**L.**
Cow. 2/9—5/10/40.**G.**
Cow. ?/?—?/1/42.**G.**
Cow. ?/?—9/4/42.**L.**
Cow. ?/?—8/8/42.**L.**
Cow. ?/?—16/9/42.**L.**
Cow. ?/?—20/8/43.**H.**
Cow. 28/6—9/8/45.**G.**
Cow. ?/?—?/11/45.**L.**
Snowplough fitted.
Cow. 12/9—1/11/47.**H.**
Cow. 12/9—2/12/49.**G.**
Cow. 14/5—16/6/51.**H/I.**
Cow. 30/3—22/4/53.**L/I.**
Cow. 7/6—3/7/54.**C/L.**
Cow. 4/1—12/2/55.**G.**
Cow. 15/4—18/5/57.**H/I.**

BOILERS:
7607.
7267 *(ex1652)* 26/3/25.
7463 *(ex4672)* 25/6/27.
7269 *(ex4662)* 9/1/32.
7269 reno. C1790 ?/?/32.
C1828 *(new)* 29/11/34.
7624 *(ex4695)* 5/10/40.
8560 *(ex4647)* 9/8/45.
9197 *(ex1761)* 2/12/49.
21180 *(ex61739)* 12/2/55.

SHEDS:
Doncaster.
St Margarets 25/1/32.
Eastfield ?/10/42.

RENUMBERED:
4686 26/3/25.
1776 13/1/46.
61776 2/12/49.

CONDEMNED: 23/3/59.
Into Cow. for cut up 17/4/59.

4687

Kitson 5337.

To traffic 6/1921.

REPAIRS:
Don. 21—29/6/21.**L.**
Don. 11—22/4/22.**L.**

Don. 6/12/22—27/4/23.**G.**
Don. 23/3—27/6/25.**G.**
Don. 31/7—14/8/25.**L.**
Don. 26/11—12/12/25.**L.**
Don. 2/2—18/3/26.**L.**
Don. 24/11/27—18/2/28.**G.**
Westinghouse brake fitted.
Don. 4/8—2/10/28.**L.**
Don. 19/7—23/8/30.**G.**
Don. 9/7—6/8/32.**G.**
Don. 20/4—1/6/35.**G.**
Don. 3/4—1/5/37.**G.**
Don. 23/9—4/11/39.**G.**
Don. 5/7—9/8/41.**G.**
Don. 2—30/10/43.**G.**
Cow. 21/10—1/12/45.**G.**
Cow. 21/4—26/6/48.**G.**
Str. 29/12/49—3/3/50.**C/L.**
Cow. 26/1—10/3/51.**H/I.**
Cow. 1/1—28/3/52.**C/L.**
Cow. 25/3—25/4/53.**G.**
Cow. 24/11—5/12/53.**C/L.**
Cow. 8/10—6/11/54.**N/C.**
Cow. 30/6—13/8/55.**L/I.**
Cow. 13/9—26/10/59.**C/L.**

BOILERS:
7608.
7264 *(ex4655)* 18/2/28.
7610 *(ex4663)* 6/8/32.
8840 *(new)* 1/6/35.
8823 *(ex4659)* 9/8/41.
8758 *(ex1778)* 26/6/48.
8758 reno. 21113 10/3/51.
21183 *(new)* 25/4/53.

SHEDS:
Doncaster.
Stratford 24/2/28.
Lowestoft 10/12/28.
Yarmouth 23/1/29.
March 1/3/30.
Cambridge 4/10/36.
Stratford 1/10/38.
March 26/4/40.
Stratford 12/1/46.
Parkeston 9/2/46.
Stratford 25/9/47.
Colwick 5/10/52.
New England 18/8/57.

RENUMBERED:
4687 27/6/25.
1777 2/2/46.
61777 26/6/48.

CONDEMNED: 11/5/59.
Into Dar. for cut up 11/7/59.

4688

Kitson 5338.

To traffic 7/1921.

REPAIRS:
Don. 20—24/12/21.**L.**
Don. 4/6—25/8/23.**G.**
Don. 6/3—30/5/25.**G.**
Don. 4—21/11/25.**L.**
Don. 18/2—20/3/26.**L.**
Don. 27/8—1/12/27.**G.**
Don. 29/2—17/3/28.**L.**
Westinghouse brake fitted.
Don. 19/10—30/11/29.**G.**
Don. 11/6—9/7/32.**G.**
Don. 23/3—13/4/35.**G.**
Don. 24/10—21/11/36.**G.**
Don. 2—30/7/38.**G.**
Don. 22/6—20/7/40.**G.**
Don. 23/1—20/2/43.**G.**
Cow. 4/3—5/5/45.**G.**
Str. 16/10—24/11/45.**L.**
Cow. 26/8—13/2/48.**G.**
Str. 8—11/11/48.**N/C.**
Cow. 30/10—12/12/50.**L/I.**
Cow. 24/3—2/5/53.**G.**
Cow. 26/8—20/10/56.**H/I.**

BOILERS:
7609.
7466 *(ex4676)* 30/11/29.
8979 *(new)* 21/11/36.
8758 *(ex4651)* 30/7/38.
8861 *(ex1768)* 13/2/48.
21184 *(new)* 2/5/53.

SHEDS:
Doncaster.
York 28/8/25.
Doncaster 2/4/26.
Stratford 17/3/28.
Southend 21/12/29.
Stratford 1/2/30.
Southend 8/3/30.
Stratford 15/3/30.
March 28/11/41.
Stratford 12/1/46.
Parkeston 21/2/46.
Stratford 25/9/47.
Lincoln 5/10/52.
Boston 13/3/55.
Lincoln 24/4/55.
Immingham 16/6/57.

RENUMBERED:
4688 30/5/25.
1778 9/2/46.
61778 12/12/50.

CONDEMNED: 9/10/59.
Sold for scrap to J.N.Connell, Coatbridge, 2/60.

4689

Kitson 5339.

To traffic 7/1921.

As built all the frames had large lightening holes between the middle and the rear wheels, and most were still so fitted to withdrawal. From August 1932 a method was devised of replacing badly worn rear portions either singly or on both sides. A new back end was butt-welded to the original front half, the joint being made between the middle and rear wheels. A strengthening plate was then riveted to the outside face and this gave a clear indication where this repair had been made. The right hand frame of No.4677 was so repaired in February 1936 but a photograph of it as No.1767 shows the left hand frame was unaltered.

Because some of those shedded at St Margarets shed worked to the Newcastle area it was required they be fitted with Raven fog signalling apparatus until October 1933 when that system went out of use. The striker can be seen just to the rear of the driving wheel. Those fitted were: 4694 (5/27 to 2/35), 4695 (8/27 to 1/35), 4696 (9/27 to 12/33), 4702 (6/27 to 4/34) and 4703 (10/27 to 10/33).

In service, all seventy-five were coupled with the GNR standard Class B, 3500 gallons tender, many of these, numbered between 5021 and 5110, were older than the engines having been built from March 1907 to September 1912. They could easily be recognised by the hand grip at the top front corner of the side sheet.

Beginning with tender No.5111, built October 1912, the top of the side sheets was extended and there was no handgrip, but the vertical handrail was made taller to match. Class B tenders were readily exchanged so both patterns could be seen coupled with individual engines.

REPAIRS:
Don. 8—13/7/21.**L.**
Don. 1—25/5/22.**L.**
Don. 8/1—3/3/23.**H.**
Don. 7/1—21/6/24.**G.**
Don. 1/3—18/4/26.**G.**
Don. 19/1—13/4/28.**G.**
Don. 19/10—12/11/29.**G.**
Don. 1/8—19/9/31.**G.**
Don. 28/11—26/12/31.**L.**
Cow. ?/?—3/6/33.**?.**
Cow. ?/?—6/10/34.**G.**
Side window cab fitted.
Cow. ?/?—16/10/34.**N/C.**
Cow. ?/?—23/3/35.**L.**
Cow. ?/?—23/4/36.**G.**
Cow. ?/?—8/7/37.**G.**
Cow. ?/?—25/8/38.**G.**
Cab screens fitted.
Cow. ?/?—23/12/39.**G.**
Cow. ?/?—31/5/41.**G.**
Hudd A.T.C. fitted.
Cow. ?/?—14/11/42.**G.**
Hudd removed.
Cow. ?/?—5/5/43.**L.**
Cow. ?/8—23/9/44.**G.**
Cow. 28/6—26/7/46.**H.**
Don. 24/1—30/4/48.**G.**
Cow. 20/10—19/11/49.**H/I.**
Cow. 11—31/5/51.**L/I.**
Cow. 28/9—20/10/51.**C/H.**
Cow. 4/11—27/12/52.**G.**
Cow. 9/10—13/11/54.**H/I.**
Cow. 25—27/11/54.**N/C.**
Cow. 20/5—22/6/57.**G.**
Cow. 27—29/6/57.**N/C.**
Cow. 21/10—14/11/58.**H/I.**
Cow. 4—18/3/59.**N/C.**

BOILERS:
7610.
7547 *(ex4645)* 13/4/28.
7547 *reno. C1789 3/6/33.*
7620 *(ex4702)* 6/10/34.
7254 *(ex4693)* 25/8/38.
9154 *(new)* 31/5/41.
9074 *(ex4641)* 23/9/44.
9074 *reno. 21148 31/5/51.*
21156 *(ex61768)* 27/12/52.
21179 *(ex61754)* 22/6/57.

SHEDS:
Doncaster.
New England 10/5/27.
Doncaster 13/4/28.
King's Cross 3/12/29.
Doncaster 24/9/31.
St Margarets 7/1/32.
Eastfield 24/4/43.
Kittybrewster 5/10/52.
Keith 7/7/54.

RENUMBERED:
4689 21/6/24.
1779 27/1/46.

61779 30/4/48.

CONDEMNED: 13/5/60.
Into Inv. for cut up 10/6/60.

4690

Kitson 5340.

To traffic 7/1921.

REPAIRS:
Don. 6—13/8/21.**L.**
Don. 11/1—3/2/23.**L.**
Don. 24/5—8/9/23.**G.**
As **1690N.**
Don. 13/6—19/9/25.**G.**
Don. 27/8—25/11/27.**G.**
Don. 29/2—17/3/28.**L.**
Altered to G.E. gauge.
Westinghouse brake fitted.
Don. 4/5—15/6/29.**G.**
Don. 27/6—1/8/31.**G.**
Don. 14/7—1/9/34.**G.**
Don. 23/5—20/6/36.**G.**
Don. 13/8—3/9/38.**G.**
Don. 17/8—28/9/40.**G.**
Don. 15/2—3/5/41.**G.**
Cow. 22/8—17/10/43.**G.**
Cow. 7—30/9/44.**L.**
Cow. 23/7—31/8/45.**L.**
Cow. 24/10—1/12/45.**L.**
Cow. 14/12/45—9/2/46.**L.**
Cow. 22/2—8/8/47.**G.**
Cow. 18/1—25/2/50.**L/I.**
Cow. 9/1—24/2/51.**H/I.**
Cow. 28/12/52—14/2/53.**G.**
Cow. 18/8—19/9/53.**C/L.**
Cow. 3/7—20/8/55.**H/I.**

BOILERS:
7611.
7464 *(ex4684)* 25/11/27.
8757 *(new)* 1/9/34.
8759 *(ex4683)* 3/9/38.
9344 *(new)* 17/10/43.
8980 *(ex1742)* 8/8/47.
8980 *reno. 21139 24/2/51.*
21175 *(ex61773)* 14/2/53.

SHEDS:
Doncaster.
Colwick ?/?
Doncaster 15/8/25.
Stratford 16/3/28.
Southend 1/2/30.
Stratford 15/2/30.
March 28/11/41.
Stratford 12/1/46.
Parkeston 21/2/46.
Stratford 25/9/47.
Colwick 5/10/52.

RENUMBERED:
4690 19/9/25.

1780 9/2/46.
61780 25/2/50.

CONDEMNED: 21/10/59.
Into Cow. for cut up 6/2/60.

4691

Kitson 5341.

To traffic 7/1921.

LOCH MORAR 8/33.

REPAIRS:
Don. 12—17/6/22.**L.**
Don. 11/1—3/2/33.**L.**
Don. 7/1—26/4/24.**G.**
Don. 7/1—18/2/25.**L.**
Altered to N.B. gauge.
Cow. ?/?—?/9/32.**?.**
Side window cab with short roof fitted.
Cow. ?/?—25/8/33.**G.**
Cow. ?/?—16/3/34.**G.**
Cow. ?/?—23/3/35.**G.**
Side window cab (with 9" extension) & drop grate fitted.
Cow. ?/?—?/6/36.**L.**
Cow. ?/?—19/10/37.**G.**
Cow. ?/?—13/5/38.**L.**
Cow. ?/?—2/9/39.**G.**
Hudd A.T.C. fitted.
Cow. ?/?—4/7/40.**L.**
Hudd removed.
Cow. ?/?—28/12/40.**G.**
Cab side screens fitted.
Hudd fitted.
Cow. ?/?—10/5/42.**L.**
Hudd removed.
Cow. ?/?—13/11/43.**G.**
Cow. ?/?—27/1/45.**G.**
Cow. ?/?—3/3/45.**L.**
Cow. ?/?—9/2/46.**L.**
Cow. 1/9—12/10/46.**G.**
Cow. 29—30/6/47.**N/C.**
Cow. 20/3—19/5/48.**G.**
Cow. 27/9—29/10/49.**L/I.**
Cow. 18/1—17/2/51.**H/I.**
Cow. 6/5—6/6/52.**L/I.**
Cow. 7/5—15/6/54.**G.**
Cow. 8/11—11/12/54.**C/L.**
Cow. 21/9—27/10/56.**L/I.**
Cow. 11—20/9/57.**C/L.**

BOILERS:
7612.
7622 *(ex4700)* 23/3/35.
9153 *(new)* 28/12/40.
9198 *(ex4635)* 27/1/45.
9347 *(ex1738)* 19/5/48.
9347 *reno. 21169 17/2/51.*
21131 *(ex61786)* 15/6/54.

SHEDS:
Doncaster.
Eastfield 23/2/25.

RENUMBERED:
4691 26/4/24.
1781 5/5/46.
61781 19/5/48.

CONDEMNED: 12/12/58.
Cut up at Kilmarnock.

4692

Kitson 5342.

To traffic 7/1921.

LOCH EIL 28/2/33

REPAIRS:
Don. 1—13/5/22.**L.**
Don. 12/2—5/5/23.**G.**
Don. 5/12/24—21/3/25.**G.**
Altered to N.B. gauge.
Cow. ?/?—18/4/31.**G.**
Cow. ?/?—28/2/33.**G.**
Cab side screens fitted.
Cow. ?/?—11/7/34.**G.**
Side window cab & drop grate fitted.
Cow. ?/?—3/1/36.**G.**
Cow. ?/?—?/9/36.**L.**
Cow. ?/?—17/11/37.**G.**
Cow. ?/?—?/7/38.**L.**
Cow. ?/?—23/12/38.**G.**
Cow. ?/?—14/2/39.**L.**
Cow. ?/?—10/2/40.**G.**
Cow. ?/?—14/6/41.**G.**
Hudd A.T.C. fitted.
Cow. ?/?—6/11/41.**L.**
Cow. ?/?—29/10/43.**H.**
Cow. ?/?—5/7/44.**L.**
Cow. 11/6—14/7/45.**G.**
Cow. ?/?—28/4/46.**L.**
Cow. ?/?—25/4/47.**N/C.**
Cow. 16/6—30/8/47.**H.**
Cow. 20/11/48—28/1/49.**H/I.**
Cow. 15/11—16/12/50.**L/I.**
Cow. ?/?—?/6/51.**C/L.**
Cow. 12/8—19/9/52.**G.**
Cow. 17/5—25/6/55.**H/I.**
Cow. 5/8—13/9/58.**G.**

BOILERS:
7613.
7605 *(ex4699)* 18/4/31.
7619 *(ex4698)* 3/1/36.
C1825 *(ex4699)* 14/6/41.
21181 *(new)* 19/9/52.
21156 *(ex61779)* 13/9/58.

SHEDS:
Doncaster.
Eastfield 27/3/25.

In 1923 ten Class B tenders had a third coal rail put on to increase capacity when used with 4-4-2 engines. No.4679 was coupled with one of these (No.5064) from 1st June 1928 to 2nd June 1934.

Ex works 18th April 1925, No.4693 had a 3-rail tender (No.5055) and took this with it to the Scottish Area when transferred 7th July 1925. During the war this tender was moved to No.4689 but from April 1947 it went to No.1781 with which it remained to 12th December 1958 withdrawal and cutting up at Kilmarnock works in January 1959.

Until June 1927 all had vacuum brake for engine, tender and train working. The ejector exhaust pipe was along the right hand side of the boiler behind the handrail and had a drain pipe just ahead of the cab.

(bottom) Although transfers to GE Section began early in 1924, the vacuum brake limited their use to fitted goods trains, because that section's passenger trains were still Westinghouse braked. Beginning with No.4664, ex works 11th June 1927, twenty - 4631, 4644, 4647, 4650, 4652, 4653, 4655, 4656, 4662, 4663, 4664, 4667, 4669, 4671, 4674, 4675, 4676, 4687, 4688, 4690 - had been fitted by April 1928 with Westinghouse as an alternative for train brakes. Note the pump was placed close to the cab. When No.4674 went for a general repair to Doncaster on 17th October 1931 it was selected for transfer to Scottish Area so the Westinghouse equipment was taken off and put on No.4677 ex works 7th November 1931.

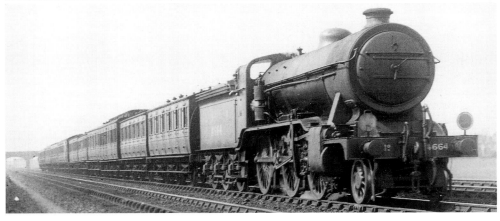

Most of the Westinghouse pumps were later moved to a more forward position. When the air brake standpipe was put on, it took the place of the vacuum pipe, which was moved to the other side of the drawhook. Note the pump exhaust had a drain pipe fitted just at its entrance to the smokebox.

Although No.4644 had its pump in the forward position when ex works 4th January 1929, on 10th August 1945 it was out with a later boiler which had two handholes, and the pump was moved nearer the cab.

Despite the need for the air brake diminishing steadily, at the end of 1951 twenty K2 were still so fitted. Nos.61737 and 61759 are believed to have still had Westinghouse fitted when withdrawn.

In June 1951 No.61734 was transferred to Scottish Region and in January 1952 it was fitted with side window cab. At that works visit the air brake equipment was removed. No others lost Westinghouse until 30th May 1953 when No.61752 had it taken off but removal then went on steadily, No.61766 being without it from 27th November 1954. Note that the vacuum standpipe was then restored to its original position.

(right) When No.4674 lost its Westinghouse in November 1931, the vacuum standpipe was moved back to the other side of the drawhook thus bringing it into line with all other braked engines.

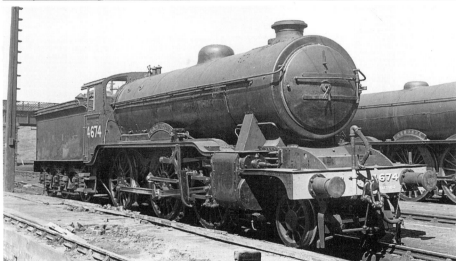

(below) Superheating was still very much on trial when this class was introduced so they were fitted with pyrometer to show degree of superheat. By Grouping, superheating was firmly established and no pyrometer was seen combined with LNER painting.

St Margarets 15/6/25.
Eastfield *by* 1/1/29.
Fort William ?/10/39.
Eastfield 1/6/52.
Kittybrewster 5/10/52.
Keith 7/7/54.

RENUMBERED:
4692 21/3/25.
1782 28/4/46.
61782 28/1/49.

CONDEMNED: 13/6/60.
Into Inv. for cut up 9/7/60.

4693

Kitson 5343.

To traffic 7/1921.

LOCH SHEIL 7/4/33

REPAIRS:
Don. 8—25/3/22.**L.**
Don. 28/11—16/12/22.**L.**
Don. 9/8—20/10/23.**G.**
Don. 19/2—18/4/25.**G.**
Don. 10—20/6/25.**L.**
Altered to N.B. gauge.
Cow. ?/?—13/6/31.**G.**
Cow. ?/?—7/4/33.**G.**
Cow. ?/?—10/9/34.**H.**
Cow. ?/?—4/12/34.**G.**
Side window cab & drop grate fitted.
Cow. ?/?—7/9/36.**G.**
Cow. ?/?—?/2/38.**L.**
Cow. ?/?—1/3/38.**G.**
Cow. ?/?—25/3/38.**N/C.**
Cow. ?/?—7/10/39.**G.**
Cow. ?/?—22/3/40.**L.**
Cab side screens fitted.
Cow. ?/?—18/1/41.**L.**
Cow. ?/?—16/8/41.**G.**
Hudd A.T.C. fitted.
Cow. ?/?—3/9/41.**L.**
Cow. 11/9—2/10/43.**G.**
Cow. ?/?—16/10/43.**L.**
Cow. 6/9—10/10/45.**G.**
Cow. 9/2—18/4/47.**H.**
Cow. 2—10/4/48.**L.**
Cow. 10/5—19/6/48.**H/I.**
Cow ?/?—?/1/49.**C/L.**
Cow. 29/7—27/8/49.**H/I.**
Cow. ?/?—?/1/51.**C/H.**
Cow. 24/9—20/10/51.**L/I.**
Cow. 18/12/54—29/1/55.**G.**
W.P.U. gear removed.
Cow. 6—19/4/55.**N/C.**
Cow. 11/2—9/3/57.**H/I.**
Cow. 18—20/3/57.**N/C.**
Cow. 1—3/4/57.**N/C.**

BOILERS:
7614.
7613 *(ex4692)* 13/6/31.
7254 *(ex4703)* 7/4/33.
9072 *(new)* 1/3/38.
7613 *(ex4685)* 2/10/43.
9475 *(ex61789)* ?/1/51.
9475 reno. 21176 20/10/51.
21116 *(ex61768)* 29/1/55.

SHEDS:
Doncaster.
Eastfield 7/7/25.
Fort William ?/10/39.
Eastfield 27/4/53.
Fort William 6/7/53.
Kittybrewster 6/6/54.
Keith 3/9/56.

RENUMBERED:
4693 18/4/25.
1783 27/1/46.
61783 10/4/48.

CONDEMNED: 17/6/59.
Sold for scrap to T.W.Ward, Wishaw, 3/8/59.

4694

Kitson 5344.

To traffic 7/1921.

REPAIRS:
Don. 27/11—16/12/22.**L.**
Don. 4/6—18/8/23.**G.**
*As **1694**ₙ.*
Don. 24/2—30/5/25.**G.**
Altered to N.B. gauge.
Cow. ?/?—?/5/27.**G.**
Cow. ?/?—3/10/31.**G.**
Cow. ?/?—?/7/34.**L.**
Cow. ?/?—20/2/35.**G.**
Side window cab fitted & fog apparatus removed.
Cow. ?/?—?/3/35.**L.**
Cow. ?/?—13/6/36.**G.**
Cow. ?/?—?/8/37.**L.**
Cow. ?/?—22/10/37.**G.**
Cow. ?/?—16/2/39.**G.**
Cab side screens.
Cow. ?/?—4/3/39.**L.**
Cow. ?/?—16/6/39.**L.**
Cow. ?/?—10/10/39.**L.**
Cow. ?/?—29/6/40.**G.**
Cow. ?/?—18/7/40.**L.**
Cow. ?/?—21/3/41.**L.**
Cow. ?/?—29/11/41.**G.**
Cow. ?/?—5/9/42.**L.**
Cow. ?/?—10/7/43.**H.**
Cow. ?/?—16/7/43.**N/C.**
Cow. ?/?—22/7/44.**L.**
Cow. ?/?—31/1/45.**L.**
Cow. 1—27/10/45.**G.**

Cow. ?/?—8/1/46.**L.**
Snow Plough.
Cow. ?/?—13/12/46.**C/L.**
Cow. 30/4—5/6/47.**H.**
Cow. 2/9—30/10/48.**H/I.**
Drop grate fitted.
Cow. 12/1—18/2/50.**G.**
Cow. ?/?—?/12/50.**N/C.**
Cow. 12/9—13/10/51.**L/I.**
Cow. 21/5—13/6/53.**L/I.**
Cow. 28/5—13/7/54.**C/L.**
Cow. 19/7—2/10/54. **C/L.**
Cow. 18—30/10/54. **C/L.**
Cow. 13/11/54. **N/C.**
Cow. 12/9—12/11/55.**G.**
Cow. 13/1—15/2/58.**H/I.**
Cow. 7—29/8/58.**C/L.**

BOILERS:
7615.
7614 *(ex4693)* 3/10/31.
C1785 *(ex4695)* 13/6/36.
C1826 *(ex4704)* 29/11/41.
8824 *(ex4684)* 27/10/45.
9011 *(ex61749)* 18/2/50.
9011 reno.21145 13/10/51.
21157 *(ex61789)* 12/11/55.

SHEDS:
Doncaster.
Eastfield 7/6/25.
St Margarets *by* 31/7/27.
Eastfield ?/10/42.
Fort William 21/5/57.

RENUMBERED:
4694 30/5/25.
1784 3/2/46.
61784 30/10/48.

CONDEMNED: 24/3/61.
Into Inv. for cut up 28/4/61.

4695

Kitson 5345.

To traffic 7/1921.

REPAIRS:
Don. 16/1—12/7/24.**G.**
Altered to N.B. gauge.
Don. 29/7—2/8/24.**L.**
Cow. ?/?—?/9/27.**G.**
Cow. ?/3—?/5/30.**G.**
Cow. ?/?—20/5/33.**G.**
Cow. ?/?—?/6/34.**L.**
Cow. ?/?—30/1/35.**G.**
Side window cab fitted & fog apparatus removed.
Cow. 7/3—7/4/36.**G.**
Cow. ?—?/4/36.**N/C.**
Cow. ?/?—29/5/37.**G.**
Cow. ?/?—?/12/37.**L.**
Cow. ?/?—25/2/38.**L.**

Cow. ?/?—24/12/38.**G.**
Cow. ?/?—6/1/39.**L.**
Cow. ?/?—12/4/39.**L.**
Cow. ?/?—11/1/40.**L.**
Cow. 1—15/6/40.**G.**
Cow. ?/?—?/2/42.**G.**
Cow. ?/?—9/5/42.**L.**
Cow. ?/?—24/10/42.**L.**
Cow. ?/?—5/2/44.**G.**
Cow. ?—12/2/44.**N/C.**
Cow. 14/5—14/6/45.**H.**
Cow. ?—27/6/45.**N/C.**
Cow. 15/3—17/4/47.**H.**
Cow. 30/7—3/12/48.**G.**
Cow. ?/?—?/3/49.**N/C.**
Cow. 7/11—14/12/50.**L/I.**
Cow. 31/3—10/5/52.**H/I.**
Cow. 13/1—13/2/54.**G.**
Cow. 16/12/54—8/1/55.**C/L.**
Cow. 22/6—15/7/55.**C/L.**
Cow. 1/8—3/9/55.**N/C.**
Cow. 10/1—16/2/57.**L/I.**
W.P.U. gear removed.

BOILERS:
7616.
C1785 *(ex4682)* 20/5/33.
7624 *(ex4701)* 7/4/36.
C1827 *(ex4701)* 15/6/40.
9073 *(ex4664)* 5/2/44.
8864 *(ex1771)* 3/12/48.
8864 reno. 21130 10/5/52.
21177 *(ex61721)* 13/2/54.

SHEDS:
New England.
Eastfield 22/12/24.
St Margarets *by* 30/8/27.
Eastfield ?/10/42.
St Margarets ?/12/42.
Eastfield 24/4/43.

RENUMBERED:
4695 2/8/24.
1785 17/2/46.
61785 3/12/48.

CONDEMNED: 23/4/59.
Cut up at Cowlairs 8/8/59.

4696

Kitson 5346.

To traffic 7/1921.

REPAIRS:
Don. 5/11/23—5/4/24.**G.**
Don. 6/1—27/2/25.**L.**
Altered to N.B. gauge.
Cow. ?/?—?/8/27.**G.**
Cow. ?/?—17/5/30.**G.**
Cow. ?/?—30/1/32.**G.**
Cow. ?/?—?/12/33.**G.**
Side window cab fitted & fog

During the 1914-18 war unlined grey livery with white numbers and letters was used but by Grouping only odd ones were still in grey as Doncaster was restoring green livery.

The twenty-five which came from NB Loco. Co. in June to September 1921 were all in standard GNR lined green passenger livery.

(below, right) After a collision No.1703 was in works from mid-October 1922 to 10th February 1923 when it came out with L&NER style green similar to No.1645 which had emerged during January in similar style. Doncaster painted no more K2's in green after No.1703 and black with red lining became the norm.

(below) Black with red lining was decreed for K2 class and until July 1923 the ampersand was included. Ten were so painted: 1689 (3/3/23), 1686 (14/4/23), 1687 (27/4/23), 1648 (4/5/23), 1666 (5/5/23), 1692 (5/5/23), 1664 (7/5/23), 1669 (16/5/23), 1641 (11/6/23), 1678 (1/7/23). Nos.1668 (11/8/23) and 1667 (18/8/23) are believed to have had only LNER but no proof has been found.

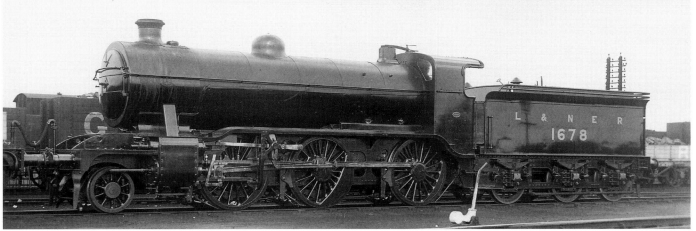

During the next six months suffix N was added to the number and was applied to: 1685ɴ (11/8/23), 1694ɴ (18/8/23), 1688ɴ (25/8/23), 1690ɴ (8/9/23), 1650ɴ (22/9/23), 1671ɴ (29/9/23), 1672ɴ (6/10/23), 1693ɴ (20/10/23), 1676ɴ (1/11/23), 1702ɴ (3/11/23), 1679ɴ (3/11/23), 1674ɴ (8/12/23), 1646ɴ (12/1/24) and 1653ɴ (19/1/24).

From the beginning of February 1924 the numbers had 3000 added and 12in. transfers on the tender were then used to February 1929.

In 1929 when Doncaster again put K2 numbers on the cab they dropped the size to 9in. to display them properly. The 12in. numbers were possible on the cab but were untidy. On the tenders 12in. letters replaced the 7½in. examples used hitherto.

apparatus removed.
Cow. ?/?—12/7/35.**G.**
Cow. ?/?—7/10/36.**G.**
Cow. ?—30/10/36.**N/C.**
Cow. ?/?—1/1/38.**G.**
Cow. ?/?—15/11/38.**G.**
Cow. ?/?—7/2/40.**L.**
Cow. ?/?—24/5/40.**G.**
Cab screens fitted.
Cow. ?/?—16/8/40.**L.**
Cow. ?/?—30/8/41.**G.**
Hudd A.T.C. fitted.
Cow. ?/?—26/9/41.**N/C.**
Cow. ?/?—12/12/42.**G.**
Hudd removed.
Cow. ?/?—4/11/43.**L.**
Cow. 4—25/11/44.**G.**
Cow. 11/5—29/6/46.**H.**
Cow. 24/10—22/11/46.**H.**
Cow. ?/?—20/5/47.**N/C.**
Cow. 14/2—6/4/48.**H/I.**
Cow. ?/?—?/12/48.**L.**
Cow. 15/11—17/12/49.**G.**
Cow. 2/1—3/2/51.**L/I.**
Cow. 8/4—15/5/52.**H/I.**
Cow. 23/2—10/4/54.**G.**
Cow. 26/4—1/5/54.**N/C.**
Cow. 29/8—1/10/55.**L/I.**
Cow. 7/7—16/8/56.**N/C.**
Cow. 9/1—8/2/58.**H/I.**

BOILERS:
7617.
7621 *(ex4700)* 17/5/30.
7684 *(ex4649)* 30/1/32.
8977 *(new)* 7/10/36.
7620 *(ex4689)* 15/11/38.
8558 *(ex4661)* 25/11/44.
8865 *(ex1732)* 17/12/49.
8865 reno. 21131 15/5/52.
21139 *(ex61780)* 10/4/54.

SHEDS:
New England.
Eastfield 2/3/25.
St Margarets *by* 27/11/27.
Eastfield ?/10/42.

RENUMBERED:
4696 5/4/24.
1786 27/1/46.
61786 6/4/48.

CONDEMNED: 7/12/59.
Sold for scrap to J.N.Connell,
Coatbridge, 2/60.

4697

Kitson 5347.

To traffic 8/1921.

LOCH QUOICH 6/33

REPAIRS:
Don. 11/1—10/5/24.**G.**
Don. 22/1—18/3/25.**L.**
Altered to N.B. gauge.
[Records incomplete]
Cow. ?/?—27/2/32.**G.**
Cow. ?/?—17/6/33.**G.**
Cow. ?/?—27/11/34.**G.**
Side window cab fitted.
Cow. ?/?—15/2/36.**G.**
Cow. 15/5—15/6/37.**G.**
Cow. ?/?—17/9/38.**L.**
Cow. ?/?—15/4/39.**L.**
Cow. ?/?—9/12/39.**G.**
Cab screens fitted.
Cow. 2—30/8/41.**G.**
Hudd A.T.C. fitted.
Cow. ?/?—25/7/43.**L.**
Cow. ?/?—11/12/43.**H.**
Cow. ?/?—18/7/45.**L.**
Cow. 8/2—16/3/46.**H.**
Cow. ?/?—3/5/47.**N/C.**
Cow. 5/11/47—24/1/48.**G.**
Cow. ?/?—19/6/48.**L/I.**
Cow. 20/6—15/8/49.**H/I.**
Cow. 31/8—24/9/49.**L/I.**
Cow. 6/3—2/6/51.**G.**
Cow. 27—29/6/51.**N/C.**
Cow. 17/12/51—28/2/52.**N/C.**
Cow. 3—20/6/53.**L/I.**
Cow. 24/1—3/3/56.**G.**
Cow. 4/2—8/3/58.**H/I.**

BOILERS:
7618.
7621 *(ex4696)* 27/2/32.
7613 *(ex4693)* 17/6/33.
8842 *(ex4703)* 15/6/37.
7619 *(ex4692)* 30/8/41.
9350 *(ex4637)* 16/3/46.
21104 *(ex61794)* 2/6/51.
21134 *(ex61762)* 3/3/56.

SHEDS:
New England.
Eastfield 1/4/25.
Fort William ?/10/39.
Eastfield 9/4/56.

RENUMBERED:
4697 10/5/24.
1787 13/1/46.
61787 19/6/48.

CONDEMNED: 29/10/59.
Sold for scrap to Arnott, Young,
Old Kirkpatrick, 17/1259.

4698

Kitson 5348.

To traffic 8/1921.

LOCH RANNOCH 7/33

REPAIRS:
Don. 19/3—5/7/24.**G.**
Altered for GE/NB gauge.
[Records incomplete]
Cow. ?/?—23/6/34.**G.**
Side window cab & drop grate
fitted.
Cow. ?/?—18/9/35.**G.**
Cow. ?/?—8/1/37.**G.**
Cow. ?/?—1/12/37.**L.**
Cow. ?/?—3/12/38.**G.**
Cow. ?/?—18/5/40.**G.**
Cab side screens fitted.
Cow. ?/?—6/7/40.**L.**
Cow. ?/?—16/11/40.**L.**
Cow. ?/?—26/12/42.**G.**
Cow. ?/?—23/6/44.**G.**
Cow. ?/?—1/7/44.**N/C.**
Cow. 14/2—30/3/46.**H.**
Cow. 18/10—26/12/47.**G.**
Cow. ?/?—18/9/48.**L/I.**
Cow. 21/10—3/12/49.**H/I.**
Cow. 8/10—3/11/51.**G.**
Cow. 3/3—16/4/52.**C/L.**
Cow. 30/3—2/5/53.**G.**
Cow. 25/12/53—29/1/54.**L/I.**
Cow. 3/7—25/8/56.**G.**
W.P.U. gear removed.
Cow. 4—8/9/56.**N/C.**
Cow. 23—24/5/57.**N/C.**
Cow. 8—19/10/57.**N/C.**
Cow. 19/9—17/10/58.**H/I.**

BOILERS:
7619.
C1826 *(new)* 23/6/34.
7684 *(ex4696)* 8/1/37.
7623 *(ex4702)* 26/12/42.
8979 *(ex1725)* 26/12/47.
21135 *(ex61753)* 3/11/51.
21109 *(ex61764)* 25/8/56.

SHEDS:
New England.
Eastfield 22/12/24.
Fort William ?/10/39.
Eastfield 27/4/53.
Fort William 6/7/53.
Eastfield 9/4/56.

RENUMBERED:
4698 5/7/24.
1788 5/5/46.
61788 18/9/48.

CONDEMNED: 26/6/61.
Into Cow. for cut up 14/11/61.

4699

Kitson 5349.

To traffic 8/1921.

LOCH LAIDON 6/34

REPAIRS:
Don. 25/2—17/5/24.**G.**
Don. 27/1—28/3/25.**L.**
Altered to N.B. gauge.
[Records incomplete]
Cow. ?/?—1/11/30.**G.**
Cow. ?/?—25/11/32.**G.**
Cow. ?/?—2/6/34.**G.**
Side window cab & drop grate
fitted.
Cow. ?/?—30/5/35.**G.**
Cow. 15/8—24/9/36.**G.**
Cow. ?/?—6/11/37.**L.**
Cow. ?/?—10/12/38.**G.**
Cow. ?/?—18/8/39.**L.**
Cow. ?/?—15/12/39.**L.**
Cab screens fitted.
Cow. ?/?—2/3/40.**L.**
Cow. 19/4—17/5/41.**G.**
Cow. ?/?—29/4/43.**G.**
Cow. ?/?—10/5/43.**L.**
Cow. ?/?—31/3/45.**G.**
Cow. ?/?—29/12/45.**L.**
Cow. 11/5—29/6/46.**G.**
Cow. ?/?—25/4/47.**N/C.**
Cow. 15/11/47—24/1/48.**H/I.**
Cow. ?/?—2/10/48.**L/I.**
Cow. ?/?—?/8/49.**C/L.**
Cow. 21/11—29/12/50.**G.**
Cow. 22/4—20/5/53.**H/I.**
Etfd. 20/7—10/8/54.**N/C.**
Cow. 10—11/8/54.**N/C.**
Cow. 26/4—28/5/55.**G.**
Cow. 6—7/7/55.**N/C.**
Cow. 4—29/12/56.**L/I.**
Cow. 6—29/3/58.**H/I.**

BOILERS:
7620.
7605 *(ex1684)* 17/5/24.
7623 *(ex4702)* 1/11/30.
C1825 *(new)* 2/6/34.
7615 *(ex4703)* 17/5/41.
9475 *(new)* 29/6/46.
9194 *(ex61764)* 29/12/50.
9194 reno. 21157 20/5/53.
21138 *(ex61745)* 28/5/55.

SHEDS:
New England.
Eastfield 1/4/25.
Fort William ?/10/39.
Eastfield 1/6/52.

RENUMBERED:
4699 17/5/24.
1789 28/4/46.
61789 2/10/48.

CONDEMNED: 30/9/59.
Into Cow. for cut up 15/12/59.

When the Scottish twenty went on to Cowlairs maintenance both letters and numbers were to their custom. Tender letters, although centred remained at 7½in., but 10in. numbers were put on the cab.

4700

Kitson 5350.

To traffic 8/1921.

LOCH LOMOND 12/33

REPAIRS:
Don. 15/4—16/8/24.**G.**
Altered for GE/NB gauge.
Cow. ?/?—30/11/29.**G.**
Cow. ?/?—24/3/33.**G.**
Cow. ?/?—?/12/33.**L.**
Cow. ?/3—14/4/34.**G.**
Side window cab & speed indicator fitted.
Cow. ?/?—24/6/35.**G.**
Cow. ?/?—?/7/35.**N/C.**
Cow. ?/?—10/11/36.**G.**
Cow. ?/?—?/1/37.**L.**
Cow. ?/?—13/9/37.**L.**
Cow. ?/?—18/2/38.**L.**
Cow. ?/?—1/10/38.**G.**
Cab side screens fitted.
Cow. ?/?—13/1/40.**L.**
Cow. ?/?—10/8/40.**G.**
Cow. 27/6—25/7/42.**G.**
Cow. ?/?—6/7/44.**H.**
Cow. ?/?—2/2/45.**L.**

Cow. ?/?—24/1/46.**L.**
Cow. 11/6—11/7/46.**H.**
Cow. ?/?—20/3/47.**L.**
Cow. 3/3—17/4/48.**G.**
Cow. 20/2—9/4/49.**L/I.**
Cow. 17/5—23/6/50.**H/I.**
Cow. ?/?—?/3/52.**C/L.**
Cow. 15/5—21/6/52.**G.**
Cow. 6/8—3/9/55.**H/I.**
W.P.U. gear removed.
Inv. 20/8—14/9/56.**C/L.**
Cow. 16/9—25/10/57.**G.**

BOILERS:
7621.
7622 *(ex4701)* 30/11/29.
7616 *(ex4695)* 14/4/34.
C1786 *(ex4702)* 1/10/38.
C1788 *(ex4674)* 25/7/42.
9072 *(ex1772)* 17/4/48.
21136 *(ex61729)* 21/6/52.
21188 *(ex61727)* 25/10/57.

SHEDS:
New England.
Eastfield 22/12/24.
Fort William ?/10/39.
Eastfield 27/4/53.
Fort William 6/7/53.
Kittybrewster 6/6/54.

RENUMBERED:
4700 16/8/24.
1790 8/9/46.
61790 17/4/48.
CONDEMNED: 3/11/59.
Sold for scrap to Arnott, Young, Old Kirkpatrick, 1/60.

4701

Kitson 5351.

To traffic 8/1921.

LOCH LAGGAN 6/5/33

REPAIRS:
Don. 11/7—8/11/24.**G.**
Don. 30/1—4/3/25.**L.**
Altered to N.B. gauge.
[Records incomplete]
Cow. 9—23/3/29.**G.**
Cow. ?/?—6/5/33.**?.**
Cow. ?/?—?/2/34.**L.**
Cow. 11/8—13/9/34.**G.**
Side window cab fitted.
Cow. ?/?—25/8/35.**G.**
Cow. ?/?—?/1/36.**L.**
Cow. ?/?—9/7/37.**G.**
Cow. ?/?—24/6/38.**L.**

Cow. ?/?—29/9/38.**G.**
Cab screens fitted.
Cow. ?/?—2/3/40.**G.**
Cow. ?/?—23/2/42.**G.**
Cow. ?/?—6/3/42.**N/C.**
Cow. ?/?—24/11/42.**L.**
Cow. ?/?—28/6/43.**L.**
Cow. ?/?—22/1/44.**G.**
Cow. ?/?—9/2/44.**N/C.**
Cow. ?/?—11/12/44.**L.**
Cow. 11/5—6/6/45.**H.**
Cow. ?/?—27/12/46.**L.**
Cow. 2/8—3/10/47.**H.**
Cow. ?/?—20/11/48.**L/I.**
Cow. 12/8—15/10/49.**G.**
Cow. 10/12/51—5/1/52.**L/I.**
Cow. ?/?—?/9/52.**C/L.**
Cow. 7/4—10/6/54.**G.**
Cow. 5—6/7/54.**N/C.**
Cow. 13/11—15/12/56.**L/I.**
Cow. 18—20/12/56.**N/C.**
Cow. 25/12/56—3/1/57.**N/C.**
Cow. 7—16/5/58.**C/L.**

BOILERS:
7622.
7624 *(ex4703)* 23/3/29.
C1827 *(new)* 13/9/34.
8977 *(ex4696)* 2/3/40.
8759 *(ex4690)* 22/1/44.

7622 *(ex1759)* 15/10/49.
7622 reno. 21102 5/1/52.
21103 *(ex61767)* 10/6/54.

SHEDS:
New England.
Eastfield 12/3/25.
St Margarets ?/1/39.
Eastfield ?/3/40.
Fort William ?/7/40.
Eastfield 27/4/53.
Fort William. 6/7/53.

RENUMBERED:
4701 8/11/24.
1791 27/7/46.
61791 20/11/48.

CONDEMNED: 22/3/60.
Into Cow. for cut up 30/4/60.

4702

Kitson 5352.

To traffic 8/1921.

REPAIRS:
Don. 7/8—3/11/23.**G.**
Don. 9/3—13/6/25.**G.**
Altered to N.B. gauge.
Don. 1—16/7/25.**L.**
Cow. ?/?—?/6/27.**G.**
Cow. ?/?—6/9/30.**G.**
Ghd. 28/10—6/11/31.**L.**
After collision with C7 2205 at Blaydon.
Cow. ?/?—12/4/34.**G.**
Side window cab fitted & fog apparatus removed.
Cow. ?/?—?/5/34.**N/C.**
Cow. ?/?—16/9/35.**G.**
Cow. ?/?—16/5/36.**C/H.**
Cow. ?/?—20/2/37.**G.**
Cow. ?/?—30/6/37.**L.**
Cow. 2—23/4/38.**G.**
Cow. ?/?—24/6/39.**G.**
Hudd A.T.C. fitted.
Cow. ?/?—2/7/39.**N/C.**
Cow. ?/?—28/12/40.**G.**
Cab side screens fitted.
Cow. 9/5—6/6/42.**G.**
Cow. ?/?—30/10/42.**L.**
Cow. ?/?—27/2/43.**L.**
Cow. ?/?—22/8/44.**G.**
Cow. ?/?—4/9/45.**L.**
Cow. 3/11—13/12/46.**H.**
Cow. ?/?—20/5/47.**N/C.**
Cow. 4/6—17/7/48.**G.**
Cow. 22—26/7/48.**L.**
Cow. 7—22/4/49.**C/L.**
Cow. 10—11/5/49.**N/C.**
Cow. 30/1—4/3/50.**H/I.**
Cow. 27/6—4/8/51.**L/I.**

Cow. 9/10—9/11/51.**C/H.**
Cow. 1—31/12/53.**L/I.**
Inv. 11/3—20/4/55.**C/L.**
Inv. 21/6—6/7/55.**N/C.**
Cow. 29/3—19/5/56.**G.**
Cow. 5/9—9/10/58.**H/I.**

BOILERS:
7623.
7620 *(ex4704)* 6/9/30.
7621 *(ex4697)* 12/4/34.
C1786 *(ex4684)* 16/5/36.
7623 *(ex4685)* 23/4/38.
8863 *(ex4651)* 6/6/42.
8863 reno. 21129 4/8/51.
21124 *(ex61775)* 9/11/51.
21120 *(ex61752)* 19/5/56.

SHEDS:
New England.
Eastfield 20/8/25.
St Margarets *by* 12/25.
Eastfield ?/10/42.
Kittybrewster 5/10/52.
Keith 7/7/54.

RENUMBERED:
4702 13/6/25.
1792 10/11/46.
61792 17/7/48.

CONDEMNED: 2/9/60.
Into Inv. for cut up 17/9/60.

4703

Kitson 5353.

To traffic 8/1921.

REPAIRS:
Don. 16/10/22—10/2/23.**H.**
After collision.
Don. 26/2—13/6/25.**G.**
Altered to N.B. gauge.
Cow. ?/7—29/10/27.**G.**
[Records incomplete]
Cow. ?/?—?/1/32.**G.**
Cow. ?/?—?/10/33.**G.**
Side window cab fitted.
Cow. ?/?—23/2/35.**G.**
Cow. ?/?—?/3/35.**L.**
Cow. ?/?—?/6/35.**L.**
Cow. ?/?—13/7/36.**G.**
Cow. 30/1—20/2/37.**C/H.**
Cow. ?/?—6/11/37.**G.**
Cow. ?/?—10/3/39.**G.**
Cow. ?/?—15/7/39.**L.**
Hudd ATC part fitted.
Cow. ?/?—20/3/41.**G.**
Hudd completed.
Cow. ?/?—14/1/43.**G.**
Hudd removed.
Cow. ?/?—23/12/44.**G.**

Cow. ?/?—23/11/45.**L.**
Cow. 18/3—3/7/47.**G.**
Cow. ?/?—?/2/48.**C/L.**
Cow. 16/5—18/6/49.**H/I.**
Cow. 8/8—16/9/50.**L/I.**
Cow. ?/?—?/12/50.**C/L.**
Cow. 12/11/51—12/1/52.**G.**
Cow. 9—28/2/53.**H/I.**
Cow. 15/11—18/12/54.**H/I.**
Cow. 17—24/8/56.**N/C.**
Cow. 11/3—20/4/57.**G.**

BOILERS:
7624.
7254 *(ex Don)* 29/10/27.
7618 *(ex4697)* ?/1/32.
8842 *(new)* 13/7/36.
7615 *(ex4682)* 20/2/37.
7622 *(ex4691)* 20/3/41.
7620 *(ex4696)* 23/12/44.
9196 *(ex1723)* 3/7/47.
9196 reno. 21159 12/1/52.
21173 *(ex61731)* 20/4/57.

SHEDS:
New England.
Eastfield 25/11/24.
Doncaster 5/1/25.
Eastfield 3/7/25.
St Margarets *by* 12/25.
Eastfield 24/4/43.
Kittybrewster 23/9/52.
Keith 7/7/54.

RENUMBERED:
4703 13/6/25.
1793 3/2/46.
61793 18/6/49.

CONDEMNED: 11/2/59.
Into Inv. for cut up 22/4/59.

4704

Kitson 5354.

To traffic 9/1921.

LOCH OICH 6/33

REPAIRS:
Don. 14/5—27/9/24.**G.**
Altered for GE/NB gauge.
[Records incomplete]
Cow. ?/?—12/7/30.**G.**
Cow. ?/?—20/10/34.**G.**
Side window cab & drop grate fitted.
Cow. ?/?—17/10/35.**L.**
Cow. ?/?—22/2/36.**G.**
Drop Grate fitted.
Cow. ?/?—26/5/37.**G.**
Cow. ?/?—2/9/38.**G.**
Cab screens fitted.
Cow. ?/?—17/6/39.**L.**

Cow. ?/?—23/3/40.**G.**
Cow. ?/?—28/9/40.**L.**
Cow. ?/?—8/11/41.**G.**
Cow. ?/?—31/10/42.**G.**
Cow. ?/?—7/12/42.**L.**
Cow. ?/?—12/8/44.**G.**
Cow. ?/?—8/2/45.**L.**
Cow. ?/?—27/10/45.**G.**
Cow. 15/9—17/10/46.**G.**
Cow. ?/?—26/6/47.**N/C.**
Cow. 11/5—2/7/48.**H/I.**
Cow. 10/3—23/4/49.**H/I.**
Cow. 22/2—19/5/51.**G.**
Cow. 2/4—1/5/54.**H/I.**
Cow. 17—26/5/54.**N/C.**
Cow. 7/2—26/3/55.**C/L.**
Cow. 8/8—1/9/56.**G.**
Cow. 21/8—19/9/58.**H/I.**

BOILERS:
7625.
7620 *(ex1699)* 27/9/24.
7617 *(ex4696)* 12/7/30.
C1789 *(ex4689)* 22/2/36.
C1826 *(ex4682)* 23/3/40.
C1828 *(ex4684)* 8/11/41.
7619 *(ex1787)* 17/10/46.
21172 *(ex61787)* 19/5/51.
21124 *(ex61792)* 1/9/56.

SHEDS:
New England.
Eastfield 22/12/24.
St Margarets 20/2/25.
Eastfield ?/27?
St Margarets ?/1/39.
Eastfield ?/7/40.

RENUMBERED:
4704 27/9/24.
1794 13/1/46.
61794 2/7/48.

CONDEMNED: 29/7/60.
Into Cow. for cut up 20/8/60.

(above) **After changing to the side window cab, Cowlairs considered this could take 12in. numbers, although the panel was the same width as before. Tender letters remained at 7½in. but from April 1936 they were changed to the standard 12in. letters.**

(left) **The white painting of the buffer beam ends in this 4th February 1941 photograph was a wartime expedient to make them a bit easier to discern in blackout conditions.**

(below) **From November 1941 red lining ceased to be put on and from July 1942 only NE was shown on the tender. This shows No.4863 with the wrong number instead of 4663.**

Captions in descending order:

Before LNER was restored the 1946 renumbering had begun and K2 class was given new numbers 1720 to 1794. No.4687 changed to 1777 at Stratford shed on Saturday 2nd February 1946 and it never had LNER restored.

No.4677, ex Doncaster on 13th April 1946 was one of the last to have a general repair at that works, and it had LNER restored, also the smaller numbers on the cab. On Sunday 13th October 1946 Parkeston shed changed it to 1767 and did so in shaded transfers of the same size.

During the war, Cowlairs not only cut to just NE but in some cases, went back to 7½in. letters. On Sunday 27th January 1946 Eastfield shed changed No.4696 to 1786 in painted numbers without any shading.

Beginning with No.1782 ex works 30th August 1947, Cowlairs applied full LNER green lined livery but without shaded transfers. Numbers and letters were in 12in. yellow paint without shading in Gill sans style but with modification to figures 6 and 9. Four more Scottish Area K2's (1791 3/10/47, 1776 1/11/47, 1764 20/11/47, 1788 26/12/47) received this livery, as did another three during early BR days (1787 24/1/48, 1789 24/1/48, 1772 27/2/48) when they might have been expected to have had the E prefix applied but Cowlairs did not take kindly to the prefix. Eventually fifteen of the twenty Scottish Area K2's were painted LNER green, the last seven with BRITISH RAILWAYS instead of LNER on the tender. The five to miss out on green livery were Nos.1774, 1779, 1784, 1785 and 1793. Only two Southern Area engines, 1732 27th September 1947 and No.1734 20th September 1947 got green livery.

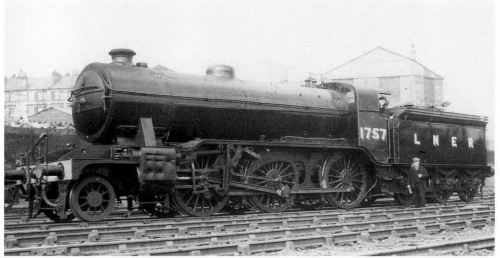

Ex works 15th August 1947, No.1757 was the last black painted LNER K2 turned out from Cowlairs and shaded transfers were available for it.

Doncaster were still doing an occasional K2 repair in early BR days and on 12th March 1948 No.E1773 was ex general repair and still in unlined black. At light repairs E1766 (18/2/48) and E1753 (20/2/48) also got the E prefix.

(below) Though still applying green lined livery, Cowlairs started to put BRITISH RAILWAYS on with No.61786 (6/4/48). Six others got this style: 61790 (17/4/48), 61781 (19/5/48), 61783 (19/6/48), 61775 (2/7/48), 61794 (2/7/48) and 61792 (17/7/48). All subsequent paintings were to black.

Of the eight in green with LNER on tender six were changed to BR number without any other alteration. Nos.61772 (1/4/48) and 61787 (19/6/48) changed whilst Cowlairs were still using 12in. figures.

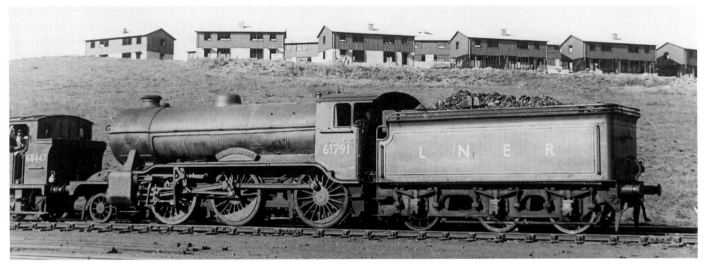

On the other four, 61788 (18/9/48), 61789 (2/10/48), 61791 (20/11/48) and 61764 (8/1/49), 10in. figures were used.

The other two in green with LNER on tender went straight to BR unlined black, 61782 (28/1/49) and 61776 (2/12/49) both still keeping modified figure 6 on the cab although it was correct on the smokebox plate.

It would seem that the Eastern Region objected to paying Cowlairs the extra cost of green painting and lining and ex Cowlairs 31st January 1948, No.1731 went back to Boston shed in unlined black and with plain tender sides. It did however get shaded transfers for its 12in. numbers.

Although No.61738 was out from a general repair on 30th April 1948 with 12in. painted numbers, Cowlairs ignored the tender and returned it still with LNER on in shaded transfers. From a light repair on 11th July 1948, No.61745 had this same style.

After heavy repairs on 26th March and 24th December 1949 (which included a change of boiler) No.61749 still went back to Colwick shed in unlined black and with no change to LNER on its tender which then survived to 10th August 1951.

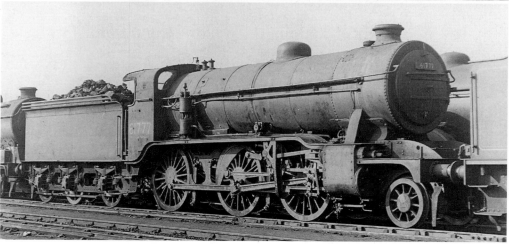

No.61777 did have its tender lettered BRITISH RAILWAYS when ex Cowlairs 26th June 1948 from a general repair. Its unlined condition survived a light repair at Stratford on 3rd March 1950 then a heavy repair at Cowlairs 10th March 1951 when the smokebox plate was added. It may even have come through a casual/ light at Cowlairs, out 28th March 1952.

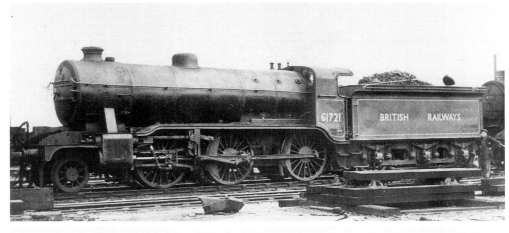

From August 1948, the standard livery was black with BR lining of red, cream, and grey, to which 61721 was favoured when ex Cowlairs 4th September 1948. The lining on the cab then restricted figure size to 10in.

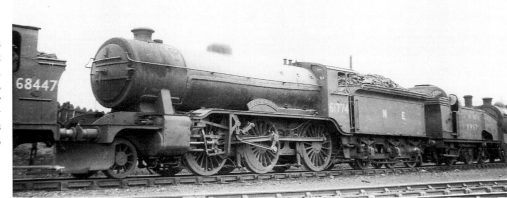

The five Scottish Area engines which were not painted green got various treatment. Ex Cowlairs on 26th June 1948 from a light repair, No.61774 had got 12in. BR number on unlined black and still with only NE on the tender. No.61793 was unlined black and with only NE when ex Cowlairs 18th June 1949.

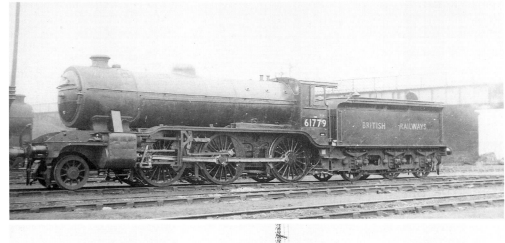

For some unknown reason No.61779's general repair of 30th April 1948 was at Doncaster. This explains why it remained in black and got 10in. numbers when Cowlairs were using green and 12in. numbers.

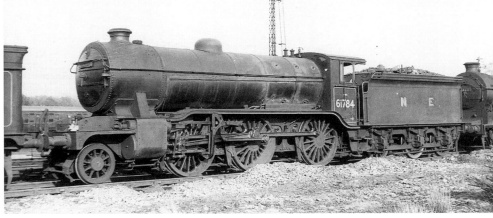

The other three were given BR lined black but out on 30th October 1948, No.61784 had unlined tender with only NE which had been put on when ex works on 27th October 1945.

Although BR standard lined livery dated from the beginning of September 1948, the first Scottish Area K2 to get it was 61785, ex Cowlairs 3rd December 1948 after a general repair.

No.61790 had lined green livery from 17th April 1948 with BRITISH RAILWAYS on the tender but as early as 9th April 1949 this was changed to black, and without any lining. Its cab figures were now 10in. instead of 12in.

When No.1788 lost the green paint and the LNER it got from 26th December 1947, this was done in two stages - from a light repair 18th September 1948 the engine returned as 61788 but in unlined black. The tender was left as it stood, with LNER on green.

The process was completed at a heavy repair from 21st October to 3rd December 1949 when BR lining was put on the engine, and the tender was repainted in black, with lining and a BR emblem.

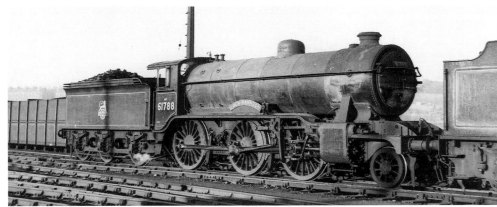

From mid-August 1949 the **BRITISH RAILWAYS** on the tender was replaced by the emblem, the 28in. size transfer being used on the K2 class. No.61766 (13/8/49) and 61774 (20/8/49), were the first of the class so treated.

Although lined black with emblem was then the standard livery, Cowlairs were still painting the modified 6 and 9.

More than half the class still had the BR emblem on the tender when they were withdrawn as shown in this 12th May 1959 photograph of No.61785, withdrawn 23rd April 1959.

The final livery change was to the BR crest from August 1957 and reported to have been applied to twenty-five of the class between 28th September 1957 (61772) and 14th November 1958 (61779). On the right hand side the lion faced the wrong way and none of the K2's had this corrected.

GNR 1641, here at Greenwood in 1921, has been fitted for oil fuel firing during the coal strike of that year. It was shedded at New England until August 1930 and was L&NER 1641 from 11th June 1923.

GNR 1682 was one of the twenty-five built by Kitson in Leeds from June to September 1921, of which fifteen started work at New England and the other ten at Doncaster. Here 1682 is on a Peterborough to London coal and goods train in 1922 south of Potters Bar.

No.1779 worked from Eastfield shed and here at Fort William is leaving for Glasgow with 1790 leading.

(left) **On Sunday 1st December 1946 No.3445 was renumbered to 1997 at Norwich shed.**

(opposite, top) **Alterations to this single engine were few and only of minor character, being limited to smokebox door and tender. From 6th November 1951 it had a door 4ft 9in. dia., curved to 6ft 5½in. radius and with hinge strap centres 15 inches apart. First it had long straps and a single door stop midway between them. Note the fresh smokebox number plate with correct 6 and 9.**

(below) **When out of Doncaster 25th August 1947 from a heavy repair, it was still unlined black but had LNER restored in yellow painted Gill sans and modified 9 in the number.**

(left) **Out from a light repair at Doncaster on 29th January 1949, and still in unlined black, it had changed to BRITISH RAILWAYS on the tender and the number to 61997 both on the cab and smokebox. The 6 and 9 were in the modified style.**

(below) **From a Doncaster general repair, ex works 30th January 1950, it was in BR lined black and with the 28 inch emblem on the tender. Note it was still sufficiently in favour to merit an official photograph. On the cab, the painted 6 and 9 were now correct Gill sans style.**

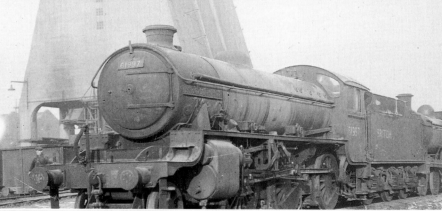

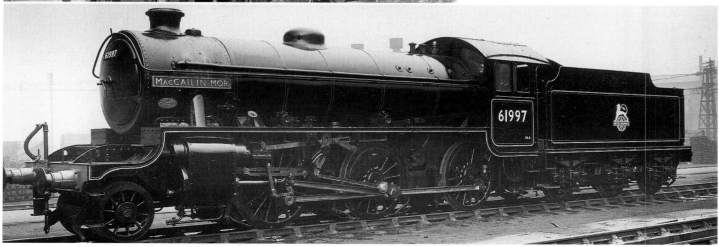

CLASS K1/1

3445

MacCAILIN MOR

Rebuilt from K4 at Doncaster.

To traffic 1/12/1945.

REPAIRS:
Don. 19—25/8/47.**H.**
Don. 14—29/1/49.**L.**
Don. 30/12/49—30/1/50.**G.**
Don. 30/12/50—17/1/51.**L/I.**
Don. 8/10—6/11/51.**H/I.**
Cow. 9—10/4/52.**N/C.**
Don. 2/1—3/2/53.**L/I.**
Don. 31/8—7/10/54.**G.**
Don. 7/5—1/6/56.**C/L.**
Cow. 29/4—1/5/57.**N/C.**
Cow. 2—5/10/57.**N/C.**
Cow. 19—21/11/57.**N/C.**
Don. 17/4—17/5/58.**G.**
Don. 10/11—9/12/58.**C/H.**
Don. 24/4/61. *Not repaired.*

BOILERS:
5054.
5054 reno.29725 6/11/51.
29684 *(ex62021)* 7/10/54.
29693 *(ex62031)* 17/5/58.

SHEDS:
New England 2/12/45.
Blaydon 16/5/46.
St Margarets 5/7/46.
Thornton Jct 6/7/46.
Eastfield 24/8/46.
Thornton Jct 1/9/46.
St Margarets 30/9/46.
Norwich 29/10/46.
New England 15/10/47.
Eastfield 13/11/49.
Fort William 24/5/54.

RENUMBERED:
1997 1/12/46.
61997 29/1/49.

CONDEMNED: 12/6/61.
Cut up at Doncaster.

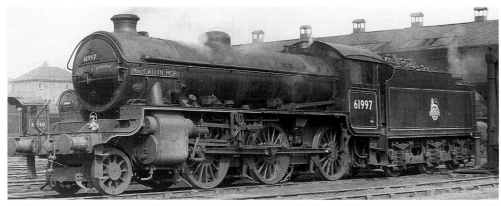

Ex works 7th October 1954 the door had been changed to one which had a cross rail, no knob, and a wheel and handle fastening. At sometime during 1957 when it had three visits to Cowlairs for non-classified repairs, it changed to a standard K1 door, with knob, two handles and a step, but no cross rail.

The tender remained the 3500 gallons type with high front plate, the only 1945 change being from vacuum to steam brake. In either October 1954 or June 1956, the division plate at the rear of the coal space was raised in height and moved 1ft 10½in. forward to prevent spillage of coal around the water filler. From its last general repair, ex Doncaster 17th May 1958, the tender emblem had been replaced by the BR crest but on the right-hand side this faced the wrong way heraldically and it was never corrected. Withdrawn 12th June 1961, Class K1/1 was then extinct.

Peppercorn took the advantage of Thompson's retirement to make some changes. The running plate in front of the cylinders was cut away to give easier access to the steam chests, and the Group Standard 4200 gallons tender was provided. On the pony truck helical instead of laminated springs were fitted. To strengthen the firebox wrapper plate ahead of the safety valves, a patch plate was put on, and this needed a raised cover plate on the boiler clothing. In 1951 five new boilers were built followed by two more in 1953 and they did not have the raised cover plate. By the later 1950's it was found that the cover plate could be done away with on the original 70 boilers and by 1960 it was no longer to be seen.

As new, the smokebox was fitted with self-cleaning apparatus of which there was no external evidence. The self-cleaning grids adversely affected ability to steam properly and new blastpipe tops with 4¾in. orifice instead of 5⅛in., and 2in. shorter were found to be needed. Indication of the apparatus was shown by fitting a small cast plate showing 'SC' on the smokebox door. Despite the difficulties posed by the self-cleaning apparatus, it remained installed and No.62024, ex works 25th April 1963, still had it.

PEPPERCORN K1 CLASS

62001

N.B.L. Co. 26605.

To traffic 30/5/1949.

REPAIRS:
Dar. 28—29/12/49.**C/L.**
Don. 15/8—18/9/51.**G.**
Don. 25—28/9/51.**N/C.**
Don. 5—11/10/51.**N/C.**
Don. 18/2—25/3/54.**G.**
Dar. 14—28/7/54.**C/L.**
Don. 14/12/54—4/1/55.**C/L.**
Dar. 8—23/6/55.**C/L.**
Don. 28/9—8/10/56.**C/L.**
Don. 27/10—5/11/56.**C/L.**
Don. 6/6—10/7/57.**G.**
Don. 5—13/6/59.**C/L.**
Don. 25/1—25/2/60.**G.**
Don. 26—28/9/60.**N/C.**
Dar. 29/11/63—7/3/64.**G.**
Dar. 9—10/3/64.**N/C.**

BOILERS:
10660.
29738 (*ex62020*) 25/3/54.
29745 (*ex62041*) 10/7/57.
29715 (*ex62018*) 25/2/60.

SHEDS:
Darlington.
Stockton 4/6/50.
Darlington 4/11/51.
Stockton 14/9/58.
Thornaby 14/6/59.
Darlington 7/4/63.
West Hartlepool 27/3/66.
York 5/2/67.

CONDEMNED: 25/4/67.
Sold for scrap to: A.Draper,
Hull, 13/7/67. Cut up 28/8/67.

62002

N.B.L. Co. 26606.

To traffic 1/6/1949.

REPAIRS:
Dar. 12—16/12/49.**C/L.**
Don. 17/7—17/8/51.**G.**
Don. 18/3—15/4/53.**G.**
Don. 19—28/5/54.**C/L.**
Dar. 25/6—3/7/54.**C/L.**
Don. 14/12/54—14/1/55.**G.**

Don. 15/11—15/12/56.**G.**
Don. 20/11—18/12/58.**G.**
Don. 21/12/60—19/1/61.**G.**
Don. 2—9/6/61.**N/C.**
Don. 14/11—7/12/62.**C/H.**
Dar. 28/5—11/9/64.**G.**

BOILERS:
10661.
29708 (*ex62033*) 15/4/53.
29715 (*ex62027*) 14/1/55.
29702 (*ex62034*) 15/12/56.
29728 (*ex62010*) 18/12/58.
29724 (*ex62065*) 19/1/61.
29714 (*ex62041*) 11/9/64.

SHEDS:
Darlington.
Heaton 25/9/49.
Blaydon 6/7/52.
Consett 6/5/62.
South Blyth 16/6/63.
North Blyth 23/10/66.

CONDEMNED: 31/10/66.
Sold for scrap to Hughes,
Bolckow, Blyth 2/67.

62003

N.B.L. Co. 26607.

To traffic 3/6/1949.

REPAIRS:
Ghd. 5—12/1/50.**C/L.**
Don. 9/8—4/9/51.**G.**
Don. 18—21/9/51.**N/C.**
Don. 9—22/10/52.**N/C.**
Don. 17/8—22/9/53.**G.**
Dar. 15—28/1/54.**C/L.**
Dar. 1—5/8/54.**C/L.**
Don. 26/8—29/9/55.**C/H.**
Don. 26/11/56—5/1/57.**G.**
Don. 25/5—3/6/59.**C/L.**
Don. 28/8—3/10/59.**G.**
Don. 19/6—9/8/62.**G.**

BOILERS:
10662.
29706 (*ex62034*) 22/9/53.
29713 (*ex62010*) 5/1/57.
29733 (*ex62007*) 3/10/59.
29726 (*ex62070*) 9/8/62.

SHEDS:
Darlington.

Heaton 25/9/49.
Darlington 6/7/52.
Stockton 14/9/58.
Thornaby 14/6/59.
Northallerton 3/4/60.
Darlington 3/3/63.

CONDEMNED: 7/6/65.
Sold for scrap to Hughes,
Bolckow, Blyth 7/65.

62004

N.B.L. Co. 26608.

To traffic 10/6/1949.

REPAIRS:
Dar. 19—20/12/49.**C/L.**
Dar. 22—28/2/51.**C/L.**
Dar. 23/9—4/10/51.**C/L.**
Don. 5/12/51—1/1/52.**G.**
Don. 28/12/53—23/1/54.**G.**
Don. 22—24/2/54.**N/C.**
Dar. 8—15/7/54.**C/L.**
Don. 3—12/3/55.**N/C.**
Dar. 16—24/6/55.**C/L.**
Don. 3/9—6/10/56.**G.**
Don. 3/9—10/10/59.**G.**
Don. 16/5—21/6/62.**G.**
Dar. 11/8/65. *Weigh.*
Dar. 23/9—17/11/65.**C/L.**

BOILERS:
10663.
10663 reno.29719 4/10/51.
29734 (*ex??*) 1/1/52.
29748 (*ex62064*) 23/1/54.
29683 (*ex62066*) 6/10/56.
29697 (*ex62064*) 10/10/59.
29707 (*ex62064*) 21/6/62.

SHEDS:
Darlington.
West Hartlepool 6/12/64.

CONDEMNED: 16/12/66.
Sold for scrap to Hughes,
Bolckow, Blyth 16/2/67.

62005

N.B.L. Co. 26609.

To traffic 10/6/1949.

REPAIRS:
Dar. 16—21/12/49.**C/L.**
Don. 28/8—26/9/51.**G.**
Don. 12/5—15/6/53.**G.**
Dar. 30/6—7/7/54.**C/L.**
Dar. 18—23/9/54.**C/L.**
Don. 18/10—12/11/55.**G.**
Don. 24/9—23/10/58.**G.**
Don. 31/10—11/11/58.**C/L.**
Don. 10—25/10/60.**N/C.**
Don. 3/1—2/2/61.**G.**
Dar. 13/11/64—23/1/65.**G.**
Dar. 25—27/1/65.**N/C.**
Dar. 2—10/2/65.**N/C.**

BOILERS:
10664.
29698 (*ex62030*) 15/6/53.
29725 (*ex61997*) 12/11/55.
29755 (*ex62015*) 23/10/58.
29730 (*ex62049*) 2/2/61.

SHEDS:
Darlington.
Heaton 25/9/49.
Darlington 6/7/52.
Ardsley 14/6/59.
York 30/8/59.
North Blyth 13/3/66.
Tyne Dock 28/5/67.
Holbeck 10/9/67.

CONDEMNED: 30/12/67.
Sold for private preservation by
Lord Garnock 30/5/69.

62006

N.B.L. Co. 26610.

To traffic 15/6/1949.

REPAIRS:
Dar. 19—21/12/49.**C/L.**
Dar. 13—20/7/51.**C/L.**
Don. 23/10—17/11/51.**G.**
Don. 4/9—8/10/53.**G.**
Dar. 28/9—6/10/54.**C/L.**
Dar. 20—23/3/55.**N/C.**
Don. 29/7—29/8/55.**G.**
Don. 10—17/8/56.**C/L.**
Don. 6—19/12/56.**C/L.**
Don. 16—18/1/57.**C/L.**
Don. 29/4—9/5/57.**C/L.**
Don. 10/10—8/11/57.**G.**
Don. 20/2—10/3/59.**C/L.**
Don. 25/4—13/5/59.**C/L.**

WORKS CODES:- Cw - Cowlairs. Dar- Darlington. Dfu - Dunfermline shed. Don - Doncaster. Etfd - Eastfied shed. Ghd - Gateshead. Gor - Gorton. Inv - Inverurie.
ThJ - Thornton Junction shed. Str - Stratford. VcA - Vickers Armstrong.
REPAIR CODES:- C/H - Casual Heavy. C/L - Casual Light. G - General. H- Heavy. H/I - Heavy Intermediate. L - Light. L/I - Light Intermediate. N/C - Non-Classified.

73

Don. 13/10—7/11/59.**G.**
Don. 15/9—13/10/61.**G.**
Don. 12/11—5/12/62.**C/H.**
Dar. 9—13/12/63.**C/L.**

BOILERS:
10665.
10665 reno.29712 20/7/51.
29726 *(ex??)* 17/11/51.
29761 *(new)* 8/10/53.
29704 *(ex62068)* 29/8/55.
29722 *(ex62044)* 8/11/57.
29749 *(ex62060)* 7/11/59.
29681 *(ex62033)* 13/10/61.

SHEDS:
Darlington.
Blaydon 31/1/54.
Gateshead 6/5/62.
Heaton 23/9/62.
Alnmouth 4/11/62.
Sunderland 19/6/66.

CONDEMNED: 4/9/66.
Sold for scrap to Hughes,
Bolckow, Blyth 12/66.

62007

N.B.L. Co. 26611.

To traffic 17/6/1949.

REPAIRS:
Dar. 25/10—14/11/49.**C/L.**
Dar. 29/12/49—4/1/50.**C/L.**
Don. 12/7—9/8/51.**G.**
Don. 21/10—5/11/52.**N/C.**
Don. 23/9—19/10/53.**G.**
Don. 26—28/4/54.**C/L.**
Dar. 19—23/10/54.**C/L.**
Don. 23/5—21/6/56.**G.**
Don. 2—9/12/57.**C/L.**
Don. 16/1—6/2/59.**C/L.**
Don. 24/4—28/5/59.**G.**
Don. 14—21/7/60.**C/L.**
Don. 31/10—29/11/61.**G.**
Don. 3—21/12/62.**C/L.**
Dar. 31/12/64—3/3/65.**H/I.**
Dar. 29/3—6/4/65.**N/C.**

BOILERS:
10666.
29703 *(ex62003)* 19/10/53.
29733 *(ex62069)* 21/6/56.
29735 *(ex62037)* 28/5/59.
29749 *(ex62006)* 29/11/61.

SHEDS:
Darlington.
Heaton 25/9/49.
Darlington 6/7/52.
York 25/8/63.
Neville Hill 28/6/64.
Sunderland 3/10/65.

Tyne Dock 23/10/66.

CONDEMNED: 9/9/67.
Sold for scrap to Hughes,
Bolckow, Blyth 9/67.

62008

N.B.L. Co. 26612.

To traffic 21/6/1949.

REPAIRS:
Dar. 9—11/1/50.**C/L.**
Dar. 14—21/8/51.**C/L.**
Don. 11/12/51—7/1/52.**G.**
Don. 30/7—25/8/54.**G.**
Don. 13/6—17/7/57.**G.**
Don. 7—13/8/58.**C/L.**
Don. 10—14/1/59.**C/L.**
Don. 7—16/10/59.**C/L.**
Don. 27/4—28/5/60.**G.**
Don. 3/1—6/2/63.**G.**

BOILERS:
10667.
29747 *(ex62042)* 25/8/54.
29705 *(ex62052)* 17/7/57.
29745 *(ex62001)* 28/5/60.
29713 *(ex62040)* 6/2/63.

SHEDS:
Darlington.
West Hartlepool 27/3/66.

CONDEMNED: 31/12/66.
Sold for scrap to Hughes,
Bolckow, Blyth 1/3/67.

62009

N.B.L. Co. 26613.

To traffic 23/6/1949.

REPAIRS:
Don. 3/1—23/3/50.**C/H.**
Dar. 27/9—4/10/50.**C/L.**
Dar. 7—14/7/51.**C/L.**
Don. 9/1—5/2/52.**G.**
Don. 16/7—6/8/53.**C/H.**
Don. 15—22/12/53.**C/L.**
Don. 24/3—15/4/54.**C/H.**
Don. 3—25/11/54.**H/I.**
Don. 27/12/57—25/1/58.**G.**
Don. 4/3—1/4/61.**G.**

BOILERS:
10668.
10668 reno.29711 14/7/51.
29719 *(ex62004)* 5/2/52.
29709 *(ex62035)* 15/4/54.
29712 *(ex62045)* 25/1/58.
29727 *(ex62050)* 1/4/61.

SHEDS:
Darlington.
Ardsley 14/6/59.
York 30/8/59.

CONDEMNED: 23/11/64.
Into Dar. for cut up 21/12/64.

62010

N.B.L. Co. 26614.

To traffic 27/6/1949.

REPAIRS:
Dar. 21—28/12/49.**C/L.**
Don. 24/7—21/8/51.**G.**
Don. 3—31/3/53.**G.**
Don. 17/2—1/3/54.**C/L.**
Don. 9—11/6/54.
Tender change.
Dar. 12—20/7/54.**C/L.**
Don. 7/12/54—5/1/55.**G.**
Ghd. 28/4—2/5/56.**C/L.**
Don. 23/10—22/11/56.**G.**
Don. 31/3—12/4/58.**C/L.**
Don. 18/8—1/10/58.**G.**
Don. 22/9—27/10/60.**G.**

BOILERS:
10669.
10669 reno.29701 21/8/51.
29689 *(ex62067)* 31/3/53.
29713 *(ex62061)* 5/1/55.
29728 *(ex62052)* 22/11/56.
29696 *(ex62024)* 1/10/58.
29701 *(ex62035)* 27/10/60.

SHEDS:
Darlington.
Heaton 25/9/49.
Blaydon 6/7/52.
North Blyth 21/1/62.
Gateshead 20/5/62.
York 8/9/63.
Goole 18/10/65.

CONDEMNED: 18/10/65.
Sold for scrap to Hughes,
Bolckow, Blyth 3/66.

62011

N.B.L. Co. 26615.

To traffic 29/6/1949.

REPAIRS:
Don. 8/11—6/12/51.**G.**
Cow. 3—9/12/53.**C/L.**
Don. 16/7—13/8/54.**G.**
Don. 19/9—15/10/55.**C/H.**
Don. 14/11—8/12/56.**H/I.**
Don. 4/6—14/7/58.**C/H.**
Don. 2/9—6/10/59.**G.**

Don. 4—26/4/61.**C/L.**
Don. 17/6—4/9/63.**G.**
Dar. 3—12/3/64.**C/L.**

BOILERS:
10670.
29691 *(ex62053)* 13/8/54.
29711 *(ex62014)* 6/10/59.
29725 *(ex62027)* 4/9/63.

SHEDS:
Gorton.
March 21/5/50.
Eastfield 10/2/52.
Fort William 1/6/52.
Alnmouth 2/12/62.
South Blyth 19/6/66.
North Blyth 23/10/66.
Tyne Dock 5/3/67.

CONDEMNED: 9/9/67.
Sold for scrap to Hughes,
Bolckow, Blyth 12/67.

62012

N.B.L. Co. 26616.

To traffic 1/7/1949.

REPAIRS:
Don. 21/5—15/6/51.**G.**
Cow. 16/5/52.**N/C.**
Don. 12/11—11/12/53.**G.**
Cow. 29/4—16/6/54.**C/L.**
Don. 14/8—21/9/56.**H/I.**
Cow. 28/2—2/3/57.**C/L.**
Cow. 30/6—2/7/58.**C/L.**
Don. 31/10—21/11/58.**C/L.**
Don. 28/10—21/11/59.**G.**
Don. 20/1—10/2/60.**C/L.**
Dar. 20/2—15/4/65.**H/I.**

BOILERS:
10671.
10671 reno.29695 15/6/51.
29699 *(ex62007)* 11/12/53.
29685 *(ex62053)* 21/11/59.
29694 *(ex62042)* 15/4/65.

SHEDS:
Gorton.
March 21/5/50.
Eastfield 10/2/52.
Fort William 1/6/52.
Alnmouth 2/12/62.
York 6/9/64.
Sunderland 30/4/67.

CONDEMNED: 17/5/67.
Sold for scrap to A.Draper,
Hull, 21/7/67. Cut up 28/8/67.

Vertical glass screens, hinged between the cab side windows, were standard equipment for crew forward lookout protection.

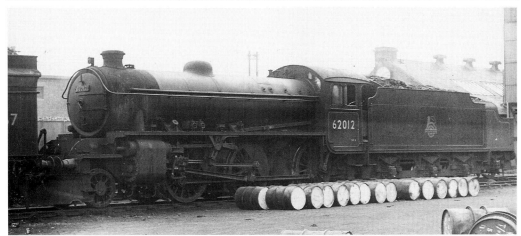

(right) In February 1952 five, Nos.62011, 62012, 62031, 62034 and 62052, were transferred from March shed to work on the West Highland line and they were adapted to carry the small type of snow-plough.

(below) Leading and driving wheels had sanding applied by steam and the boxes had the Downs' small bore steam coil in them to keep the sand dry and free flowing.

(above) **On the prototype only the leading sandbox filler had a raised cap and angled backing plate. Nos.62001 to 62070 also had this filler arrangement for both pairs of boxes. Despite some difficulties with leaking steam coils from vibration, the Downs' type sanding was retained through to withdrawal.**

(left) **All seventy had full electric lighting provided from a Stone's steam turbine driven generator at the right hand side of the smokebox. Unlike some of the other classes which had this type of electric lighting taken off, all K1 class seem to have retained it to withdrawal.**

(below) **When new, all were fitted with B.T.H. speed indicator, driven off the left hand trailing crank pin, with the bracket attached to the running plate.**

62013

N.B.L. Co. 26617.

To traffic 4/7/1949.

REPAIRS:
Str. 10—17/10/50.C/L.
Don. 1—24/1/52.G.
Don. 10/3—9/4/54.G.
Don. 10—30/11/54.C/H.
Don. 1—29/3/56.G.
Don. 22/10—12/11/56.C/H.
Don. 13/6—22/7/58.G.
Don. 17/3—20/4/61.G.

BOILERS:
10672.
29711 (ex62069) 9/4/54.
29721 (ex62056) 30/11/54.
29748 (ex62004) 29/3/56.
29742 (ex62032) 12/11/56.
29758 (ex62029) 22/7/58.
29708 (ex62066) 20/4/61.

SHEDS:
Gorton.
March 21/5/50.
Stratford 9/12/58.
Frodingham 24/1/60.

CONDEMNED: 29/10/63.
Sold for scrap to Bulwell Forest
Wagon Works 7/64.

62014

N.B.L. Co. 26618.

To traffic 5/7/1949.

REPAIRS:
Don. 6/3—4/4/51.G.
Don. 14/1—5/2/53.G.
Don. 9—19/8/54.C/L.
Don. 8/12/54—7/1/55.G.
Don. 23/5—22/6/57.G.
Don. 13/6—21/7/59.G.
Don. 22/2—24/3/62.G.
Don. 30/11—20/12/62.C/L.

BOILERS:
10673.
29756 (new) 4/4/51.
29757 (ex62023) 5/2/53.
29697 (ex62037) 7/1/55.
29711 (ex62030) 22/6/57.
29706 (ex62025) 21/7/59.
29689 (ex62018) 24/3/62.

SHEDS:
Gorton.
March 14/5/50.
Stratford 14/9/58.
March 21/9/58.

Stratford 14/12/58.
Frodingham 31/1/60.
Doncaster 4/11/62.
Frodingham 10/1/65.

CONDEMNED: 6/6/65.
Sold for scrap to T.W.Ward,
Killamarsh 9/65.

62015

N.B.L. Co. 26619.

To traffic 7/7/1949.

REPAIRS:
Don. 2—6/10/50.C/L.
Don. 19/9—12/10/51.G.
Don. 22/4—5/5/52.C/H.
Don. 1—20/4/53.N/C.
Don. 6/1—2/2/54.G.
Don. 11/6—9/7/54.C/L.
Don. 17/9—11/10/54.C/L.
Don. 12/6—17/7/56.G.
Don. 31/8—7/9/57.C/L.
Don. 24/7—22/8/58.G.
Don. 11/7—3/8/61.G.

BOILERS:
10674.
10674 reno.29707 12/10/51.
29746 (ex??) 5/5/52.
29737 (ex62017) 2/2/54.
29755 (ex62026) 17/7/56.
29750 (ex62026) 22/8/58.
29746 (ex62039) 3/8/61.

SHEDS:
Gorton.
March 21/5/50.
Stratford 14/12/58.
March 10/9/61.
Retford 24/9/61.
Doncaster 4/11/62.
Frodingham 10/1/65.

CONDEMNED: 25/7/65.
Sold for scrap to A.Draper,
Hull, 10/65. Cut up 8/11/65.

62016

N.B.L. Co. 26620.

To traffic 8/7/1949.

REPAIRS:
Don. 28/8—1/12/50.C/H.
Don. 21/3—5/4/51.C/L.
Don. 5/12/51—4/1/52.G.
Don. 20/11—19/12/53.G.
Don. 30/9—8/10/54.C/L.
Don. 2/12/55—5/1/56.G.
Don. 25/2—11/3/57.C/H.
Don. 23/4—21/5/58.G.

Don. 25/7—27/8/60.G.

BOILERS:
10675.
10675 reno.29683 1/12/50.
29735 (ex??) 4/1/52.
29692 (ex62037) 19/12/53.
29718 (ex62059) 5/1/56.
29757 (ex62025) 11/3/57.
29688 (ex62052) 21/5/58.
29741 (ex62036) 27/8/60.

SHEDS:
Gorton.
March 21/5/50.
Frodingham 11/12/60.

CONDEMNED: 13/7/63.
Into Don. for cut up 13/1/64.

62017

N.B.L. Co. 26621.

To traffic 12/7/1949.

REPAIRS:
Don. 24/8—18/9/50.C/L.
Don. 14—22/11/50.C/L.
Don. 12/12/51—10/1/52.G.
Don. 17/12/53—15/1/54.G.
Don. 23/7—9/8/54.C/L.
Don. 29/4—12/5/55.C/L.
Don. 27/1—29/2/56.G.
Don. 20/5—19/6/58.G.
Don. 25/4—27/6/60.G.
Don. 10/10—23/11/62.G.
Dar. 26/10—1/12/65.C/L.

BOILERS:
10676.
10676 reno.29681 22/11/50.
29737 (ex??) 10/1/52.
29727 (ex62036) 15/1/54.
29732 (ex62054) 29/2/56.
29731 (ex62047) 19/6/58.
29686 (ex62040) 27/6/60.
29733 (ex62003) 23/11/62.

SHEDS:
Gorton.
March 21/5/50.
Frodingham 11/12/60.
North Blyth 10/10/65.

CONDEMNED: 20/2/67.
Sold for scrap to Hughes,
Bolckow, Blyth 26/4/67.

62018

N.B.L. Co. 26622.

To traffic 13/7/1949.

REPAIRS:
Don. 17—28/7/50.C/L.
Don. 2/5—8/6/51.G.
Don. 13/3—10/4/53.G.
Don. 9—19/8/54.C/L.
Don. 17/3—15/4/55.G.
Don. 22/12/55—3/1/56.N/C.
Don. 18/1—16/2/57.G.
Don. 4—12/10/57.C/L.
Don. 26/2—6/3/58.C/L.
Don. 18—23/4/58.C/L.
Don. 10/6—11/7/59.G.
Don. 15/11—20/12/61.G.
Don. 26/11—12/12/62.C/H.

BOILERS:
10677.
10677 reno.29694 8/6/51.
29701 (ex62010) 10/4/53.
29688 (ex62067) 15/4/55.
29715 (ex62002) 16/2/57.
29689 (ex62039) 11/7/59.
29723 (ex62037) 20/12/61.

SHEDS:
Gorton.
March 14/5/50.
Frodingham 3/1/60.

CONDEMNED: 13/3/64.
Into Don. for cut up 20/3/64.

62019

N.B.L. Co. 26623.

To traffic 15/7/1949.

REPAIRS:
Don. 21—23/8/50.C/L.
Don. 16/10—8/11/51.G.
Don. 17—27/3/52.C/L.
Don. 14/1—9/2/54.G.
Don. 2—20/9/54.C/L.
Don. 23/11—17/12/55.G.
Don. 29/8—26/9/56.C/L.
Don. 19/2—20/3/58.G.
Don. 24/5—30/6/60.G.
Don. 2—23/11/62.C/H.

BOILERS:
10678.
29734 (ex62004) 9/2/54.
29726 (ex62035) 17/12/55.
29698 (ex62040) 20/3/58.
29717 (ex62021) 30/6/60.

SHEDS:
Gorton.
March 21/5/50.
Cambridge 18/5/52.
March 25/5/52.
Stratford 9/12/58.
March 10/9/61.
Retford 17/9/61.

CONDEMNED: 2/7/64.
Sold for scrap to T.W.Ward
Killamarsh 10/64.

62020

N.B.L. Co. 26624.

To traffic 1/8/1949.

REPAIRS:
Don. 28—29/8/50.**C/L**.
Don. 1—26/10/51.**G**.
Don. 3—23/1/52.**C/H**.
Don. 30/4—21/5/52.**C/L**.
Don. 13—20/8/52.**N/C**.
Don. 4—24/2/54.**G**.
Don. 7—15/10/54.**C/L**.
Don. 16/12/55—18/1/56.**G**.
Don. 18/2—15/3/58.**G**.
Don. 11/11—5/12/59.**G**.
Don. 10/10—20/11/62.**G**.

BOILERS:
10679.
29738 (ex??) 23/1/52.
29746 (ex62015) 24/2/54.
29761 (ex62006) 18/1/56.
29716 (ex62062) 15/3/58.
29683 (ex62004) 5/12/59.
29759 (ex62047) 20/11/62.

SHEDS:
Gorton.
Brunswick 2/10/49.
Gorton 16/10/49.
March 21/5/50.
Frodingham 10/1/60.

CONDEMNED: 10/1/65.
Sold for scrap to: A.Draper,
Hull, 2/65. Cut up 10/6/65.

62021

N.B.L. Co. 26625.

To traffic 2/8/1949.

REPAIRS:
Ghd. 21—23/11/49.**C/L**.
Don. 20/3—13/4/51.**G**.
Don. 30/9—27/10/52.**G**.
Don. 11/8—15/9/54.**G**.
Don. 11/7—18/8/56.**G**.
Don. 17—19/7/57.**C/L**.
Ghd. 24—26/2/58.**N/C**.
Don. 24/3—24/4/58.**G**.
Don. 12/2—12/3/60.**G**.
Don. 18/1—17/2/62.**G**.

BOILERS:
10680.
29759 (new) 13/4/51.
29684 (ex62037) 27/10/52.

29744 (ex62045) 15/9/54.
29717 (ex62061) 24/4/58.
29718 (ex62054) 12/3/60.
29750 (ex62015) 17/2/62.

SHEDS:
Blaydon.
Gateshead 6/5/62.
Alnmouth 25/11/62.
Sunderland 19/6/66.
Tyne Dock 23/10/66.

CONDEMNED: 30/10/66.
Sold for scrap to A.Draper,
Hull, 4/67. Cut up 29/5/67.

62022

N.B.L. Co. 26626.

To traffic 4/8/1949.

REPAIRS:
Ghd. 10—17/11/49.**C/L**.
Don. 13/3—6/4/51.**G**.
Don. 18—27/4/51.**N/C**.
Don. 13/10—10/11/52.**G**.
Don. 29/7—24/8/54.**G**.
Don. 8/8—6/9/56.**G**.
Don. 29/9—24/10/58.**G**.
Don. 31/12/59—21/1/60.**C/L**.
Don. 28/11/60—3/1/61.**G**.
Don. 5—27/11/62.**C/H**.
Don. 9/7—5/9/63.**G**.
Dar. 8/1—13/2/65.**C/H**.

BOILERS:
10681.
29758 (new) 6/4/51.
29755 (ex62054) 10/11/52.
29707 (ex62029) 24/8/54.
29727 (ex62017) 6/9/56.
29680 (ex62038) 24/10/58.
29744 (ex62038) 3/1/61.
29711 (ex62011) 5/9/63.

SHEDS:
Blaydon.
Consett 6/5/62.
North Blyth 12/5/63.

CONDEMNED: 4/9/66.
Sold for scrap to Hughes,
Bolckow, Blyth 11/66.

62023

N.B.L. Co. 26627.

To traffic 5/8/1949.

REPAIRS:
Don. 11—21/11/49.**C/L**.
Ghd. 6—10/7/50.**C/L**.
Dar. 16/10—10/11/50.**C/L**.

Don. 26/2—28/3/51.**G**.
Don. 16/12/52—8/1/53.**G**.
Don. 2—29/7/54.**G**.
Don. 4/4—9/5/56.**G**.
Don. 26/4—29/5/58.**G**.
Don. 13—18/7/59.**N/C**.
Don. 16/8—20/9/60.**G**.
Don. 4/12/62—4/1/63.**G**.

BOILERS:
10682.
29757 (new) 28/3/51.
29758 (ex62022) 8/1/53.
29729 (ex62049) 29/7/54.
29720 (ex62055) 9/5/56.
29729 (ex62035) 29/5/58.
29684 (ex62069) 20/9/60.
29722 (ex62044) 4/1/63.

SHEDS:
Blaydon.
Consett 6/5/62.
Heaton 23/9/62.
Alnmouth 4/11/62.
Sunderland 19/6/66.
Tyne Dock 23/10/66.

CONDEMNED: 26/6/67.
Sold for scrap to Garnham,
Harris & Elton, Chesterfield,
9/67.

62024

N.B.L. Co. 26628.

To traffic 8/8/1949.

REPAIRS:
Ghd. 9—16/1/50.**C/L**.
Don. 28/3—20/4/51.**G**.
Don. 30/12/52—23/1/53.**G**.
Don. 23—26/2/53.**N/C**.
Don. 30/9—28/10/54.**G**.
Ghd. 21—27/4/56.**C/L**.
Don. 20/6—1/8/56.**G**.
Don. 28/7—30/8/58.**G**.
Don. 1/6—8/7/60.**G**.
Don. 13/3—25/4/63.**G**.

BOILERS:
10683.
29759 (ex62021) 23/1/53.
29723 (ex62062) 28/10/54.
29696 (ex62036) 1/8/56.
29721 (ex62070) 30/8/58.
29698 (ex62019) 8/7/60.
29686 (ex62017) 25/4/63.

SHEDS:
Blaydon.
Gateshead 6/5/62.
North Blyth 28/2/65.

CONDEMNED: 13/2/67.
Sold for scrap to Hughes,
Bolckow, Blyth 24/4/67.

62025

N.B.L. Co. 26629.

To traffic 10/8/1949.

REPAIRS:
Ghd. 28/11—2/12/49.**C/L**.
Don. 28/3—14/4/50.**C/L**.
Dar. 28/11—8/12/50.**C/L**.
Don. 14/6—13/7/51.**G**.
Don. 16/4—11/5/53.**G**.
Dar. 22—29/7/54.**C/L**.
Don. 5/1—1/2/55.**G**.
Don. 15/1—9/2/57.**G**.
Don. 26—28/8/57.**C/L**.
Don. 13—20/8/58.**C/L**.
Don. 8—10/10/58.**C/L**.
Don. 25/2—26/3/59.**G**.
Don. 1—29/4/61.**G**.

BOILERS:
10684.
29700 (ex62002) 11/5/53.
29757 (ex62014) 1/2/55.
29706 (ex62003) 9/2/57.
29737 (ex62030) 26/3/59.
29756 (ex62061) 29/4/61.

SHEDS:
Blaydon.
North Blyth 21/1/62.
Gateshead 20/5/62.
Heaton 23/9/62.
Alnmouth 4/11/62.
North Blyth 19/6/66.
Tyne Dock 29/1/67.

CONDEMNED: 10/4/67.
Sold for scrap to Arnott Young,
Dinsdale 13/7/67.

62026

N.B.L. Co. 26630.

To traffic 11/8/1949.

REPAIRS:
Ghd. 9—18/11/49.**C/L**.
Dar. 30/1—17/2/51.**C/L**.
Don. 25/4—23/5/51.**G**.
Don. 9/10—7/11/52.**G**.
Dar. 28/3—2/4/53.**N/C**.
Dar. 11—18/12/53.**N/C**.
Don. 27/8—1/10/54.**G**.
Don. 5/6—13/7/56.**G**.
Don. 16/6—24/7/58.**G**.
Don. 30/3—29/4/60.**G**.
Don. 7/5—9/6/62.**G**.
Don. 11—31/10/62.**C/H**.

In the later 1950's the speed indicator was taken off most of the class, as was the driving link, but on the majority the bracket was left in place.

A few did also have the speed indicator bracket taken off, Nos.62002 and 62007 being so noted. From August 1963 No.62007 had a B1 class tender, and the others paired with a B1 tender were 62020, 62045, 62046, 62063 and 62066.

As delivered by N.B. Loco. Co. all had smokebox number plate already fitted and they differed noticeably from those cast in BR workshops by the figures being spaced closer. Through to 62070 they included the modified 6 and 9 but a large proportion of the class later received standard BR plates as shown on 62007 in the previous photograph. Some engines kept the original plate until withdrawal (*see* 62024 on page 72).

Dar. 29/3/65. *Weigh.*

BOILERS:
10685.
29722 (*ex62063*) 7/11/52.
29755 (*ex62022*) 1/10/54.
29750 (*ex62068*) 13/7/56.
29732 (*ex62017*) 24/7/58.
29748 (*ex62046*) 29/4/60.
29718 (*ex62021*) 9/6/62.

SHEDS:
Blaydon.
Gateshead 6/5/62.
Sunderland 28/2/65.
Tyne Dock 23/10/66.
North Blyth 29/1/67.
Sunderland 14/5/67.
West Hartlepool 28/5/67.

CONDEMNED: 1/7/67.
Sold for scrap to Arnott Young,
Dinsdale 7/67.

62027

N.B.L. Co. 26631.

To traffic 15/8/1949.

REPAIRS:
Ghd. 22—25/11/49.**C/L**.
Don. 30/7—23/8/51.**G**.
Don. 22/4—15/5/53.**G**.
Dar. 20—26/6/54.**C/L**.
Don. 17/11—16/12/54.**G**.
Don. 1/11—1/12/56.**G**.
Don. 27/11—7/12/57.**C/L**.
Don. 14/10—18/11/58.**G**.
Don. 27/10—26/11/60.**G**.
Don. 8—16/6/61.**C/L**.
Don. 10/4—5/6/63.**G**.

BOILERS:
10686.
29715 (*ex62037*) 15/5/53.
29714 (*ex62044*) 16/12/54.
29707 (*ex62022*) 1/12/56.
29725 (*ex62005*) 18/11/58.
29745 (*ex62008*) 5/6/63.

SHEDS:
Blaydon.
Consett 6/5/62.
North Blyth 23/5/65.

CONDEMNED: 20/3/67.
Sold for scrap to Arnott Young,
Dinsdale 4/7/67.

62028

N.B.L. Co. 26632.

To traffic 17/8/1949.

REPAIRS:
Ghd. 5—8/12/49.**C/L**.
Don. 3—24/4/51.**G**.
Don. 9—15/5/51.**N/C**.
Don. 4/9—9/10/52.**G**.
Don. 4/8—2/9/54.**G**.
Don. 20/2—22/3/56.**G**.
Don. 21/1—13/2/58.**G**.
Don. 19—26/2/58.**N/C**.
Don. 10/3—14/4/60.**G**.
Don. 5/12/62—11/1/63.**G**.

BOILERS:
10687.
29685 (*ex62051*) 9/10/52.
29758 (*ex62023*) 2/9/54.
29740 (*ex62050*) 22/3/56.
29743 (*ex62056*) 13/2/58.
29716 (*ex62020*) 14/4/60.
29734 (*ex62054*) 11/1/63.

SHEDS:
Blaydon.
Gateshead 6/5/62.
York 8/9/63.

CONDEMNED: 21/11/66.
Sold for scrap to Arnott Young,
Parkgate & Rawmarsh 9/2/67.

62029

N.B.L. Co. 26633.

To traffic 19/8/1949.

REPAIRS:
Ghd. 17—23/1/50.**C/L**.
Dar. 5—7/2/51.**N/C**.
Don. 16/4—17/5/51.**G**.
Don. 25/9—20/10/52.**G**.
Don. 15/6—21/7/54.**G**.
Don. 7/3—7/4/56.**G**.
Dar. 30/7—6/9/57.**C/L**.
Don. 19/5—18/6/58.**G**.
Don. 4—10/2/59.**C/L**.
Don. 17/5—10/6/60.**G**.

BOILERS:
10688.
29707 (*ex62015*) 20/10/52.
29710 (*ex62038*) 21/7/54.
29758 (*ex62028*) 7/4/56.
29720 (*ex62023*) 18/6/58.
29731 (*ex62017*) 10/6/60.

SHEDS:
Blaydon.
Gateshead 6/5/62.
York 8/9/63.

CONDEMNED: 5/10/64.
Sold for scrap to A.Draper,
Hull, 11/64. Cut up 9/12/64.

62030

N.B.L. Co. 26634.

To traffic 22/8/1949.

REPAIRS:
Ghd. 30/12/49—6/1/50.**C/L**.
Don. 20/6—23/7/51.**G**.
Don. 30/3—24/4/53.**G**.
Ghd. 1—8/12/53.**C/L**.
Dar. 4—9/8/54.**C/L**.
Don. 19/1—18/2/55.**G**.
Don. 3—9/4/56.**C/L**.
Don. 27/12/56—24/1/57.**G**.
Don. 16/12/58—17/1/59.**G**.
Don. 31/12/60—28/1/61.**G**.

BOILERS:
10689.
29694 (*ex62018*) 24/4/53.
29711 (*ex62013*) 18/2/55.
29737 (*ex62015*) 24/1/57.
29702 (*ex62002*) 17/1/59.
29680 (*ex62022*) 28/1/61.

SHEDS:
Blaydon.
Gateshead 6/5/62.
Alnmouth 4/11/62.
Sunderland 28/2/65.

CONDEMNED: 9/8/65.
Sold for scrap to Hughes,
Bolckow, Blyth 12/65.

62031

N.B.L. Co. 26635.

To traffic 24/8/1949.

REPAIRS:
Don. 12—24/1/50.**C/L**.
Don. 24/4—18/5/51.**G**.
Don. 31/7—10/8/51.**N/C**.
Don. 3—22/1/52.**L/I**.
Don. 7/8—6/9/52.**H/I**.
Cow. 14/5/54.**N/C**.
Don. 11/11—3/12/54.**G**.
Don. 10—24/10/55.**C/L**.
Don. 23/5—22/6/56.**C/L**.
Don. 26/2—14/4/58.**G**.
Don. 26/5—16/7/60.**C/L**.
ATC mech only fitted.

BOILERS:
10690.
29693 (*ex62054*) 3/12/54.
29761 (*ex62020*) 14/4/58.

SHEDS:
March.
Eastfield 17/2/52.
Fort William 24/5/54.

CONDEMNED: 29/12/62.
Into Cow. for cut up 20/3/64.

62032

N.B.L. Co. 26636.

To traffic 26/8/1949.

REPAIRS:
Don. 12—20/12/49.**C/L**.
Don. 27/10—8/11/50.**C/L**.
Don. 14/11—12/12/51.**G**.
Don. 23/5—5/6/52.**C/L**.
Don. 31/3—28/4/54.**G**.
Don. 24/11—3/12/54.**C/L**.
Don. 15/12/54—3/1/55.**C/L**.
Don. 29/8—5/10/56.**G**.
Don. 14—25/5/57.**C/L**.
Don. 6—15/1/58.**G**.
Don. 11—19/4/58.**C/L**.
Don. 1—12/7/58.**C/L**.
Don. 3/12/58—7/1/59.**G**.
Don. 3/2—3/3/61.**G**.

BOILERS:
10691.
29742 (*ex62068*) 28/4/54.
29746 (*ex62020*) 5/10/56.
29692 (*ex62055*) 7/1/59.
29736 (*ex62057*) 3/3/61.

SHEDS:
March.
Frodingham 17/1/60.

CONDEMNED: 7/9/63.
Sold for scrap to Bulwell Forest
Wagon Works 1/64.

62033

N.B.L. Co. 26637.

To traffic 31/8/1949.

REPAIRS:
Don. 24—26/1/50.**C/L**.
Don. 16—20/10/50.**C/L**.
Don. 24/4—23/5/51.**G**.
Don. 16/5—3/6/52.**C/H**.
Don. 27/2—23/3/53.**G**.
Don. 24/8—3/9/54.**C/L**.
Don. 18/1—15/2/55.**G**.
Don. 13—26/3/56.**C/L**.
Don. 9/3—6/4/57.**G**.
Don. 3/3—7/4/59.**G**.
Don. 9/8—13/9/61.**G**.

BOILERS:
10692.
29708 (*ex62020*) 3/6/52.
29756 (*ex62014*) 23/3/53.
29700 (*ex62025*) 15/2/55.
29723 (*ex62024*) 6/4/57.

29681 *(ex62042)* 7/4/59.
29755 *(ex62005)* 13/9/61.

SHEDS:
March.
Frodingham 18/12/60.

CONDEMNED: 10/1/65.
Sold for scrap to A.Draper,
Hull, 3/65. Cut up 27/4/65.

62034

N.B.L. Co. 26638.

To traffic 1/9/1949.

REPAIRS:
Don. 21/12/49—11/1/50.**C/L**.
Don. 18/9—11/10/51.**G**.
Don. 2/7—5/8/53.**G**.
Don. 22/11—11/12/54.**C/L**.
Don. 2/6—10/7/56.**G**.
Don. 9—23/1/58.**C/L**.
Don. 20/7—13/8/60.**C/L**.
ATC mech only fitted.
Don. 24/10—3/11/60.**C/L**.
Cow. 29/12/60—5/1/61.**N/C**.
Cow. 16—18/2/61.**N/C**.
Don. 14/11/61. *Not repaired*
and stored unserviceable
from 20/11/61.

BOILERS:
10693.
29702 *(ex62027)* 5/8/53.
29703 *(ex62007)* 10/7/56.

SHEDS:
March.
Eastfield 17/2/52.
Fort William 24/5/54.

CONDEMNED: 29/12/62.
Cut up at Doncaster.

62035

N.B.L. Co. 26639.

To traffic 7/9/1949.

REPAIRS:
Don. 12—19/1/50.**C/L**.
Don. 2/10—9/11/51.**G**.
Don. 5/11—2/12/53.**G**.
Don. 27/4—3/5/54.**C/L**.
Don. 12—28/7/54.**C/L**.
Don. 13/1—4/2/55.**C/L**.
Don. 18/5—9/6/55.**C/H**.
Don. 8/5—7/6/56.**G**.
Don. 11—19/7/56.**C/L**.
Don. 10/4—9/5/58.**G**.
Don. 27/5—2/7/60.**G**.
Don. 9/1—25/2/63.**G**.

BOILERS:
10694.
29726 *(ex62006)* 2/12/53.
29739 *(ex62053)* 9/6/55.
29729 *(ex62023)* 7/6/56.
29701 *(ex62036)* 9/5/58.
29700 *(ex62058)* 2/7/60.
29683 *(ex62020)* 25/2/63.

SHEDS:
March.
Frodingham 18/12/60.

CONDEMNED: 18/7/65.
Sold for scrap to A.Draper,
Hull, 10/65. Cut up 8/11/65.

62036

N.B.L. Co. 26640.

To traffic 9/9/1949.

REPAIRS:
Don. 28—31/3/50.**C/L**.
Don. 24/10—17/11/51.**G**.
Don. 30/9—20/10/52.**C/L**.
After collision.
Don. 21/10—13/11/53.**G**.
Don. 17—31/8/54.**C/L**.
Don. 15/11—14/12/55.**G**.
Don. 31/12/55—3/1/56.**N/C**.
Don. 5—14/3/57.**C/L**.
Don. 18—21/6/57.**C/L**.
Don. 13—21/8/57.**C/L**.
Don. 26/2—28/3/58.**G**.
Don. 27/2—5/3/59.**C/L**.
Don. 25/3—23/4/60.**G**.

BOILERS:
10695.
29696 *(ex62039)* 13/11/53.
29701 *(ex62018)* 14/12/55.
29741 *(ex62067)* 28/3/58.
29738 *(ex62044)* 23/4/60.

SHEDS:
March.
Cambridge 11/3/51.
March 8/4/51.
Stratford 9/12/58.
Doncaster 8/1/61.

CONDEMNED: 26/10/63.
Into Don. for cut up 2/11/63.

62037

N.B.L. Co. 26641.

To traffic 14/9/1949.

REPAIRS:
Don. 25/4—3/5/50.**C/L**.
Don. 20/11/50—15/2/51.**C/H**.

Don. 29/6—17/7/51.**C/L**.
Don. 29/8—2/10/52.**G**.
Don. 25/11—15/12/52.**C/H**.
Don. 8—22/5/53.**C/H**.
Don. 28/10—23/11/54.**G**.
Don. 13/12/56—19/1/57.**G**.
Don. 21/3—25/4/59.**G**.
Don. 18/10—18/11/61.**G**.

BOILERS:
10696.
10696 reno.29684 15/2/51.
29715 *(ex62065)* 2/10/52.
29692 *(ex62026)* 15/12/52.
29697 *(ex62025)* 22/5/53.
29760 *(ex62051)* 23/11/54.
29735 *(ex62038)* 19/1/57.
29723 *(ex62033)* 25/4/59.
29739 *(ex62060)* 18/11/61.

SHEDS:
March.
Stratford 19/2/61.
March 10/9/61.
Retford 8/10/61.
Doncaster 4/11/62.

CONDEMNED: 26/12/64.
Sold for scrap to Hughes,
Bolckow, Blyth 3/65.

62038

N.B.L. Co. 26642.

To traffic 16/9/1949.

REPAIRS:
Don. 19/12/49—18/1/50.**C/L**.
Don. 1/5—9/11/50.**C/H**.
Don. 11—29/12/50.**C/L**.
Don. 31/7—23/8/51.**C/L**.
Don. 5/6—10/7/52.**G**.
Don. 22/3—14/4/54.**G**.
Don. 16—25/11/54.**C/L**.
Don. 8—24/2/55.**C/L**.
Don. 16—24/11/55.**C/L**.
Don. 5—24/1/56.**C/L**.
Don. 24/7—25/8/56.**G**.
Don. 5—19/3/58.**C/L**.
Don. 24/8—2/10/58.**G**.
Don. 21/11—17/12/60.**G**.
Don. 26/11—14/12/62.**C/H**.

BOILERS:
10697.
10697 reno.29682 9/11/50.
29710 *(ex62059)* 10/7/52.
29735 *(ex62016)* 14/4/54.
29680 *(ex62070)* 25/8/56.
29744 *(ex62021)* 2/10/58.
29729 *(ex62023)* 17/12/60.

SHEDS:
March.

Doncaster 8/4/62.

CONDEMNED: 16/10/63.
Sold for scrap to J. Rigley &
Sons, Bulwell Forest 30/1/64.

62039

N.B.L. Co. 26643.

To traffic 22/9/1949.

REPAIRS:
Don. 12—19/1/50.**C/L**.
Don. 2—30/5/51.**G**.
Don. 12/2—9/3/53.**G**.
Don. 3—22/12/53.**C/H**.
Don. 27/8—14/9/54.**C/L**.
Don. 3/2—4/3/55.**G**.
Don. 28/9—3/11/56.**H/I**.
Don. 25/1—2/2/57.**C/L**.
Don. 5—13/5/58.**C/L**.
Don. 21/1—21/2/59.**G**.
Don. 13/2—16/3/61.**G**.
Don. 4—28/12/61.**C/L**.
Don. 10/5/62. *Weigh.*

BOILERS:
10698.
29696 *(ex62053)* 9/3/53.
29750 *(ex62054)* 22/12/53.
29689 *(ex62010)* 4/3/55.
29746 *(ex62032)* 21/2/59.
29747 *(ex62045)* 16/3/61.

SHEDS:
March.
Cambridge 11/3/51.
March 1/4/51.
Retford 29/4/62.

CONDEMNED: 14/12/63.
Into Don. for cut up 23/1/64.

62040

N.B.L. Co. 26644.

To traffic 3/10/1949.

REPAIRS:
Don. 21/12/49—13/1/50.**C/L**.
Don. 9—16/10/50.**C/L**.
Don. 19/1—8/2/52.**G**.
Don. 5—12/5/52.**N/C**.
Don. 7—31/12/53.**G**.
Don. 14—22/10/54.**C/L**.
Don. 29/11—28/12/55.**G**.
Don. 8—16/11/56.**C/L**.
Don. 24/5—3/6/57.**C/L**.
Don. 14/11—11/12/57.**G**.
Don. 21/8—1/9/59.**C/L**.
Don. 20—29/10/59.**C/L**.
Don. 12/1—5/2/60.**G**.
Don. 6—20/5/60.**N/C**.

There was appreciable changing of smokebox doors and thus variation in type. The previous photograph shows the standard had straps little more than half way across and each had a stop at the hinged end. Four, Nos.62016, 62026, 62050 and 62058 changed to this type with longer straps and a single door stop between the hinges.

Nos.62008 and 62011 were also noted with a door which had straps on 2ft instead of 15in. centres, and on these the number plate was below the top strap and not above it.

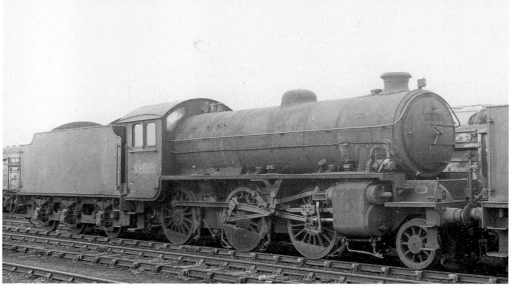

A hopper ashpan was provided with the door being operated by turning a key below the frame on the right hand side. The operating implement was easily and often lost, so in later years a fixed handle was fitted.

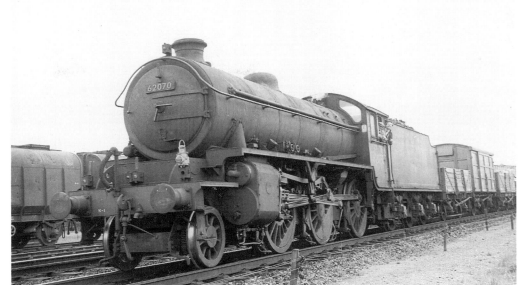

The hopper ashpan was in two portions so a fixed operating handle was also fitted on the left hand side.

Change of complete smokebox was not unusual and No.62015 had one at Doncaster in 1954.

From new, carriage heating apparatus, with connection also at the front end, was provided. Note self cleaning smokebox indication is now absent in this May 1964 photograph.

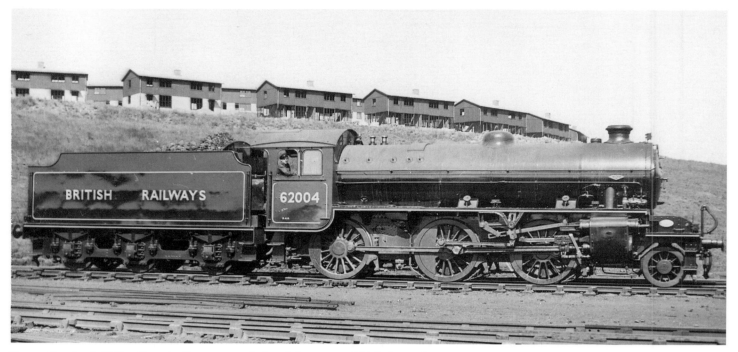

Group Standard 4200 gallons tender was coupled and they were of high front plate type, and welded instead of riveted.

Until the mid-1950's the rear division plate was of the same height as the side plates, and was only just in front of the water filler.

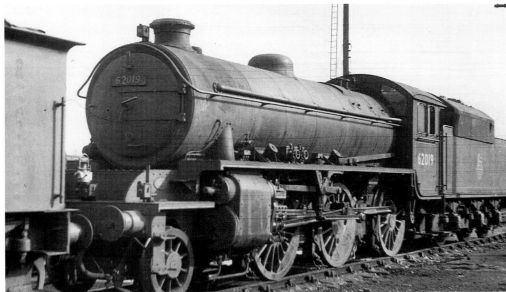

(above) **From about 1955 the rear division plate was raised to match the front plate and was moved 1ft 10½in. forward.**

(right) **Until April 1952, No.62019 was coupled with a standard tender with which it came from the makers. On 8th April that year it took over a coal-weighing tender from 62015 and on 24th May regained a normal K1 tender.**

Other K1's to have coal weighing tender were Nos.62010 (3/54 to 6/54), 62015 (29/3/52 to 8/4/52), 62020 (25/4/52 to 30/4/52). All four duly regained normal type tenders; 62010, 62015 and 62019 getting K1 welded type but 62020 got a B1 riveted type.

Don. 4—30/8/61.**C/L.**
Don. 1/10—13/11/62.**G.**

BOILERS:
10699.
29695 *(ex62012)* 31/12/53.
29698 *(ex62005)* 28/12/55.
29686 *(ex62049)* 11/12/57.
29713 *(ex62003)* 5/2/60.
29748 *(ex62026)* 13/11/62.

SHEDS:
March.
Retford 8/10/61.
Doncaster 4/11/62.

CONDEMNED: 10/1/65.
Sold for scrap to A.Draper,
Hull, 2/65. Cut up 3/6/65.

62041

N.B.L. Co. 26645.

To traffic 5/10/1949.

REPAIRS:
Dar. 18—19/1/50.**C/L.**
Dar. 18—25/9/51.**C/L.**
Don. 19/3—18/4/52.**G.**
Don. 27/7—19/8/54.**L/I.**
Don. 29/4—1/6/57.**G.**
Don. 20/10—17/11/60.**G.**
Don. 22/10—20/11/62.**C/H.**
Dar. 12/6—19/9/64.**G.**

BOILERS:
10700.
10700 reno.29718 25/9/51.
29745 *(ex??)* 18/4/52.
29714 *(ex62027)* 1/6/57.
29724 *(ex62002)* 19/9/64.

SHEDS:
Darlington.
Stockton 12/2/50.
Thornaby 14/6/59.
Darlington 26/7/59.
West Hartlepool 27/3/66.

CONDEMNED: 10/4/67.
Sold for scrap to ??, 13/7/67.

62042

N.B.L. Co. 26646.

To traffic 7/10/1949.

REPAIRS:
Dar. 22—24/5/50.**C/L.**
Dar. 24/7—1/8/51.**C/L.**
Don. 16/6—18/7/52.**G.**
Don. 30/6—26/7/54.**G.**
Don. 17/10—14/11/56.**C/L.**

Don. 1—4/12/56.**C/L.**
Don. 19/9—18/10/58.**G.**
Don. 4—30/1/60.**C/L.**
Don. 1/4—3/5/61.**G.**
Dar. 19/1—12/3/65.**H/I.**

BOILERS:
10701.
29681 *(ex62066)* 26/7/54.
29682 *(ex62066)* 18/10/58.
29694 *(ex62048)* 3/5/61.
29727 *(ex62009)* 12/3/65.

SHEDS:
Darlington.
Stockton 12/2/50.
Thornaby 14/6/59.
York 17/6/62.
Sunderland 30/4/67.
West Hartlepool 28/5/67.

CONDEMNED: 1/7/67.
Sold for scrap to Arnott Young,
Dinsdale 10/67.

62043

N.B.L. Co. 26647.

To traffic 10/10/1949.

REPAIRS:
Dar. 6—8/7/50.**C/L.**
Dar. 8—15/8/51.**C/L.**
Dar. 1—4/4/52.**N/C.**
Don. 1—29/7/52.**G.**
Dar. 17—19/7/54.**C/L.**
Don. 23/2—16/3/55.**C/L.**
Don. 1/5—2/6/56.**G.**
Don. 25/5—18/6/59.**G.**
Don. 22/12/61—20/1/62.**G.**

BOILERS:
10702.
29682 *(ex62038)* 29/7/52.
29734 *(ex62019)* 2/6/56.
29687 *(ex62050)* 18/6/59.
29757 *(ex62059)* 20/1/62.

SHEDS:
Darlington.
Stockton 12/2/50.
Ardsley 16/6/57.
Darlington 15/9/57.

CONDEMNED: 12/7/65.
Sold for scrap to Geo. Cohen,
Cargo Fleet, 9/65.

62044

N.B.L. Co. 26648.

To traffic 13/10/1949.

REPAIRS:
Dar. 23—26/5/50.**C/L.**
Dar. 14—21/9/51.**C/L.**
Don. 12/2—7/3/52.**G.**
Don. 13/1—1/2/54.**C/L.**
Don. 6/10—3/11/54.**G.**
Don. 7—31/5/56.**C/L.**
Don. 18/9—16/10/57.**G.**
Don. 3/3—1/4/60.**G.**
Don. 19/9—6/11/62.**G.**
Dar. 25/10—28/11/63.**N/C.**
Cow. ?/?—16/5/66.**C/H.**

BOILERS:
10703.
10703 reno.29717 21/9/51.
29714 *(ex62048)* 7/3/52.
29722 *(ex62026)* 3/11/54.
29738 *(ex62001)* 16/10/57.
29722 *(ex62006)* 1/4/60.
29697 *(ex62004)* 6/11/62.
29685 *(ex62012)* 16/5/66.

SHEDS:
Darlington.
Northallerton 17/5/53.
Darlington 3/3/63.
West Hartlepool 27/3/66.

CONDEMNED: 1/7/67.
Sold for scrap to Arnott Young,
Dinsdale 10/67.

62045

N.B.L. Co. 26649.

To traffic 14/10/1949.

REPAIRS:
Dar. 23—26/5/50.**C/L.**
Dar. 19—27/12/51.**C/L.**
Don. 11/3—2/4/52.**G.**
Dar. 12—20/1/54.**C/L.**
Don. 8/7—5/8/54.**G.**
Don. 18—27/10/56.**C/L.**
Don. 17—28/12/56.**C/L.**
Don. 3—30/8/57.**G.**
Don. 7—11/10/57.**C/L.**
Don. 21/7—1/8/59.**C/L.**
Don. 1—17/10/59.**C/L.**
Don. 5/10—4/11/60.**G.**
Don. 21/3—13/4/61.**C/L.**
Dar. 9/9—2/11/63.**G.**
Cow. ??—?/?66.**?.**

BOILERS:
10704.
10704 reno.29723 27/12/51.
29744 *(ex??)* 2/4/52.
29712 *(ex62047)* 5/8/54.
29747 *(ex62008)* 30/8/57.
29695 *(ex62062)* 4/11/60.

SHEDS:
Darlington.
West Hartlepool 27/3/66.
Tyne Dock 2/7/67.

CONDEMNED: 9/9/67.
Sold for scrap to Hughes,
Bolckow, Blyth 9/67.

62046

N.B.L. Co. 26650.

To traffic 21/10/1949.

REPAIRS:
Dar. 8—18/5/50.**C/L.**
Don. 5—29/2/52.**G.**
Don. 16/7—13/8/54.**G.**
Dar. 30/9—2/10/56.**C/L.**
Don. 12/4—11/5/57.**G.**
Don. 17/12/59—20/1/60.**G.**
Don. 10—13/10/60.**N/C.**
Don. 19—22/9/61.**C/L.**
Dar. 15/10—30/11/63.**G.**
Dar. 2—5/12/63.**N/C.**

BOILERS:
10705.
29719 *(ex62009)* 13/8/54.
29748 *(ex62013)* 11/5/57.
29691 *(ex62011)* 20/1/60.
29744 *(ex62022)* 30/11/63.

SHEDS:
Darlington.
York 10/6/56.

CONDEMNED: 12/2/67.
Sold for scrap to Hughes,
Bolckow, Blyth 24/4/67.

62047

N.B.L. Co. 26651.

To traffic 20/10/1949.

REPAIRS:
Dar. 6—9/3/50.**C/L.**
Dar. 25—27/1/51.**C/L.**
Dar. 20—28/7/51.**C/L.**
Don. 12/11—5/12/51.**G.**
Don. 20/5—10/6/53.**C/L.**
Dar. 28/2—3/3/54.**C/L.**
Don. 10/6—14/7/54.**G.**
Don. 12—23/2/57.**C/L.**
Don. 10/2—7/3/58.**G.**
Don. 17/10—1/11/60.**N/C.**
Don. 2—27/5/61.**G.**
Don. 31/7—16/8/61.**C/L.**

BOILERS:
10706.
29712 *(ex62006)* 5/12/51.

All had steam brake on engine and tender with vacuum ejector for train braking.

During the 1960's a few of the class were fitted with BR Automatic Warning System. Note 62002 lost both its speedometer bracket and also all its electric lighting equipment.

29731 (ex62032) 14/7/54.
29759 (ex62048) 7/3/58.
29728 (ex62002) 27/5/61.

SHEDS:
Darlington.
York 10/6/56.
Darlington 14/9/58.
Stockton 23/11/58.
Low Moor 14/6/59.
York 30/8/59.

CONDEMNED: 1/3/65.
Sold for scrap to A.Draper,
Hull, 4/65. Cut up 24/5/65.

62048

N.B.L. Co. 26652.

To traffic 21/10/1949.

REPAIRS:
Dar. 2—4/5/50.C/L.
Dar. 17—24/8/51.C/L.
Dar. 19—21/9/51.N/C.
Don. 28/1—21/2/52.G.
Dar. 28/6—3/7/54.C/L.
Don. 1/12/54—6/1/55.G.
Don. 3—19/1/57.C/L.
Don. 13/12/57—10/1/58.G.
Don. 1/9—3/10/58.C/L.
Don. 9/11—7/12/60.G.
Don. 22/10—13/11/62.C/H.
Dar. 9/9—26/11/63.G.
Don. 20/11/64—13/1/65.C/L.
After collision.

BOILERS:
10707.
10707 reno.29714 24/8/51.
29741 (ex??) 21/2/52.
29759 (ex62024) 6/1/55.
29694 (ex62063) 10/1/58.
29704 (ex62063) 7/12/60.

SHEDS:
Darlington.
Heaton 19/11/50.
Darlington 1/1/51.
Haverton Hill 2/9/51.
York 10/6/56.
Darlington 1/11/59.
West Hartlepool 13/3/66.

CONDEMNED: 19/6/67.
Sold for scrap to Garnham,
Harris & Elton, Chesterfield,
8/67.

62049

N.B.L. Co. 26653.

To traffic 25/10/1949.

REPAIRS:
Dar. 2—4/10/50.C/L.
Dar. 28/7—3/8/51.C/L.
Don. 7—29/11/51.G.
Don. 22/4—20/5/54.G.
Dar. 17—21/10/54.C/L.
Don. 8—16/2/57.C/L.
Don. 17/10—9/11/57.G.
Don. 23/8—1/10/60.G.
Don. 25/10—5/11/60.N/C.
Don. 17/4—16/5/61.C/L.

BOILERS:
10708.
29686 (ex62024) 20/5/54.
29730 (ex62057) 9/11/57.
29705 (ex62008) 1/10/60.

SHEDS:
Darlington.
Heaton 19/11/50.
Darlington 1/1/51.
Heaton 22/1/51.
Darlington 17/6/51.
York 10/6/56.

CONDEMNED: 14/6/65.
Sold for scrap to Hughes,
Bolckow, Blyth 8/65.

62050

N.B.L. Co. 26654.

To traffic 28/10/1949.

REPAIRS:
Dar. 30/8—6/9/51.C/L.
Don. 23/1—15/2/52.G.
Don. 4/6—7/7/53.C/L.
Don. 14/6—14/7/54.C/L.
Don. 9/8—1/9/55.G.
Don. 2/12/58—3/1/59.G.
Don. 1/2—2/3/61.G.
Don. 26/3—17/5/63.G.

BOILERS:
10709.
29687 (ex62063) 1/9/55.
29727 (ex62022) 3/1/59.
29702 (ex62030) 2/3/61.
29716 (ex62028) 17/5/63.

SHEDS:
Darlington.
Heaton 19/11/50.
Darlington 1/1/51.
Heaton 22/1/51.
Darlington 17/6/51.
Haverton Hill 7/10/51.
York 10/6/56.
Blaydon 1/11/59.
Consett 6/5/62.
Alnmouth 1/11/64.
North Blyth 19/6/66.

Tyne Dock 5/3/67.

CONDEMNED: 9/9/67.
Sold for scrap to Hughes,
Bolckow, Blyth 9/67.

62051

N.B.L. Co. 26655.

To traffic 3/11/1949.

REPAIRS:
Don. 29/12/50—15/3/51.C/H.
Don. 22/8—25/9/52.G.
Don. 21—27/11/52.N/C.
Don. 28/7—18/8/53.C/H.
Don. 1/9—7/10/54.G.
Don. 13—24/9/55.C/L.
Don. 4—14/7/56.C/L.
Don. 20/2—21/3/57.G.
Don. 30/4—30/5/59.G.
Don. 11/5—10/6/61.G.

BOILERS:
10710.
29720 (ex62064) 25/9/52.
29760 (new) 18/8/53.
29685 (ex62028) 7/10/54.
29760 (ex62037) 21/3/57.
29742 (ex62013) 30/5/59.
29737 (ex62025) 10/6/61.

SHEDS:
March.
Retford 13/5/62.
Doncaster 4/11/62.

CONDEMNED: 10/1/65.
Sold for scrap to A.Draper,
Hull, 2/65. Cut up 22/3/65.

62052

N.B.L. Co. 26656.

To traffic 4/11/1949.

REPAIRS:
Don. 21/2—3/3/50.C/L.
Don. 7—17/11/50.C/L.
Don. 2—26/11/51.G.
Don. 28/5—21/7/53.G.
Don. 27/10—10/11/53.C/L.
Don. 2/11—2/12/55.C/L.
Cow. 29/3—7/4/56.C/L.
Cow. 4—8/5/56.N/C.
Don. 25/5—22/6/57.G.
Don. 26/2—20/3/58.C/H.
Don. 7/3—6/4/60.G.
ATC mech only fitted.

BOILERS:
10711.
29705 (ex62005) 21/7/53.

29688 (ex62018) 22/6/57.
29740 (ex62028) 20/3/58.
29699 (ex62012) 6/4/60.

SHEDS:
March.
Eastfield 17/2/52.
Fort William 24/5/54.

CONDEMNED: 29/12/62.
Into Cow. for cut up 9/4/64.

62053

N.B.L. Co. 26657.

To traffic 8/11/1949.

REPAIRS:
Don. 21/5—20/6/51.G.
Don. 20/2—17/3/53.G.
Don. 9/6—5/7/54.C/H.
Don. 31/3—30/4/55.G.
Don. 25/5—3/7/57.G.
Don. 27/8—1/10/59.G.

BOILERS:
10712.
29691 (ex62033) 17/3/53.
29739 (ex62040) 5/7/54.
29756 (ex62033) 30/4/55.
29685 (ex62051) 3/7/57.
29760 (ex62051) 1/10/59.

SHEDS:
March.
Stratford 9/12/58.
Doncaster 8/1/61.

CONDEMNED: 24/12/63.
Into Don. for cut up 7/2/64.

62054

N.B.L. Co. 26658.

To traffic 11/11/1949.

REPAIRS:
Don. 19/12/50—8/3/51.C/H.
Don. 10/9—10/10/52.G.
Don. 10—12/12/52.N/C.
Don. 10—26/3/53.C/H.
Don. 18/2—10/3/54.C/H.
Don. 23/9—4/10/54.C/L.
Don. 30/12/54—21/1/55.G.
Don. 7—10/3/55.N/C.
Don. 12/6—6/7/56.C/L.
Don. 29/4—1/6/57.G.
Don. 14/7—11/8/59.G.
Don. 4/5—8/6/62.G.

BOILERS:
10713.
29755 (new) 8/3/51.

29750 (ex??) 10/10/52.
29693 (ex62039) 26/3/53.
29732 (ex62055) 10/3/54.
29690 (ex62031) 21/1/55.
29718 (ex62016) 1/6/57.
29734 (ex62043) 11/8/59.
29706 (ex62014) 8/6/62.

SHEDS:
March.
Retford 8/10/61.

CONDEMNED: 20/12/64.
Sold for scrap to Hughes,
Bolckow, Blyth 2/65.

62055

N.B.L. Co. 26659.

To traffic 17/11/1949.

REPAIRS:
Don. 5—8/6/50.**C/L.**
Don. 20/11—18/12/51.**G.**
Don. 20/1—15/2/54.**G.**
Don. 29/10—11/11/54.**C/L.**
Don. 29/9—11/10/55.**C/L.**
Don. 13/1—16/2/56.**G.**
Don. 15—22/6/57.**C/L.**
Don. 9/7—6/8/58.**G.**
Don. 15/9—15/10/60.**G.**
Don. 7—30/11/62.**C/H.**

BOILERS:
10714.
29720 (ex62051) 15/2/54.
29692 (ex62016) 16/2/56.
29690 (ex62054) 6/8/58.

SHEDS:
March.
Doncaster 25/3/62.

CONDEMNED: 26/12/64.
Sold for scrap to Hughes,
Bolckow, Blyth 2/65.

62056

N.B.L. Co. 26660.

To traffic 24/11/1949.

REPAIRS:
Dar. 5—8/6/50.**C/L.**
Dar. 16—23/1/52.**C/L.**
Don. 10/7—12/8/52.**G.**
Don. 28/9—27/10/54.**G.**
Don. 19/7—13/8/56.**C/L.**
Don. 14/8—6/9/57.**G.**
Don. 3—18/2/58.**C/L.**
Don. 21/11—23/12/60.**G.**

BOILERS:
10715.
10715 reno.29724 23/1/52.
29721 (ex62062) 12/8/52.
29743 (ex62058) 27/10/54.
29719 (ex62046) 6/9/57.

SHEDS:
Darlington.
Haverton Hill 7/1/51.
York 10/6/56.

CONDEMNED: 18/5/65.
Sold for scrap to M.Baum,
Cleveland Dock, Middlesbrough
7/65.

62057

N.B.L. Co. 26661.

To traffic 30/11/1949.

REPAIRS:
Dar. 7—10/3/51.**C/L.**
Don. 25/2—21/3/52.**G.**
Don. 1—15/10/53.**C/L.**
Don. 19—27/11/53.**C/L.**
Don. 12/8—14/9/54.**G.**
Don. 5—31/10/57.**G.**
Don. 4—20/8/59.**C/L.**
Don. 28/3—8/4/60.**C/L.**
Don. 4—28/10/60.**G.**
Dar. 6/4—13/6/64.**G.**
Dar. 15—16/6/64.**N/C.**

BOILERS:
10716.
29717 (ex62044) 21/3/52.
29730 (ex62011) 14/9/54.
29736 (ex62058) 31/10/57.
29696 (ex62010) 28/10/60.

SHEDS:
Darlington.
Haverton Hill 7/1/51.
York 10/6/56.
North Blyth 13/3/66.

CONDEMNED: 1/5/67.
Sold for scrap to Arnott Young,
Dinsdale 13/7/67.

62058

N.B.L. Co. 26662.

To traffic 6/12/1949.

REPAIRS:
Dar. 25—28/1/51.**C/L.**
Dar. 14—21/7/51.**C/L.**
Don. 19/2—13/3/52.**G.**
Don. 24/8—28/9/54.**G.**
Don. 18—24/1/57.**C/L.**

Don. 6/7—3/8/57.**G.**
Don. 10/5—4/6/60.**G.**
Don. 9/11—2/12/60.**C/L.**
Don. 23/1—5/3/63.**C/L.**

BOILERS:
10717.
10717 reno.29713 21/7/51.
29743 (ex??) 13/3/52.
29736 (ex62008) 28/9/54.
29700 (ex62033) 3/8/57.
29732 (ex62026) 4/6/60.

SHEDS:
Darlington.
Haverton Hill 2/9/51.
Stockton 16/6/57.
Darlington 8/6/58.
York 18/8/63.

CONDEMNED: 3/8/64.
Sold for scrap to A.Draper,
Hull, 11/64. Cut up 23/11/64.

62059

N.B.L. Co. 26663.

To traffic 13/12/1949.

REPAIRS:
Dar. 1—4/8/50.**C/L.**
Dar. 1—6/3/51.**N/C.**
Dar. 7—14/7/51.**C/L.**
Don. 13/5—6/6/52.**G.**
Dar. 7—10/7/54.**C/L.**
Don. 10/1—7/2/55.**G.**
Don. 4—15/3/57.**C/L.**
Don. 5/5—6/6/58.**G.**
Don. 27/5—1/7/61.**G.**
Don. 27—30/3/62.**C/L.**
Dar. 24/7—10/10/64.**G.**
Dar. 12—14/10/64.**N/C.**
Dar. 19—22/10/64.**N/C.**
Dar. 29/10—5/11/64.**N/C.**
Dar. 18/11/64. Weigh.
Cow. ?/?—22/9/66.**C/H.**

BOILERS:
10718.
10718 reno.29710 14/7/51.
29718 (ex62041) 6/6/52.
29708 (ex62002) 7/2/55.
29757 (ex62016) 6/6/58.
29758 (ex62013) 1/7/61.

SHEDS:
Darlington.
Haverton Hill 2/9/51.
Ardsley 16/6/57.
Darlington 15/9/57.
Northallerton 27/3/60.
Darlington 21/8/60.
North Blyth 20/2/66.

CONDEMNED: 12/2/67.
Sold for scrap to Hughes,
Bolckow, Blyth 24/4/67.

62060

N.B.L. Co. 26664.

To traffic 20/12/1949.

REPAIRS:
Dar. 20/6—31/8/50.**C/L.**
Ghd. 14—21/7/51.**C/L.**
Don. 18/8—22/9/52.**G.**
Dar. 1—5/8/54.**C/L.**
Don. 16/3--4/4/55.**C/L.**
Don. 3/7—9/8/56.**G.**
Don. 23/5—18/6/59.**G.**
Don. 8/4—13/5/61.**G.**
Dar. 6/1—18/3/64.**G.**

BOILERS:
10719.
29739 (ex62068) 18/6/59.
29712 (ex62009) 13/5/61.
29720 (ex62065) 18/3/64.

SHEDS:
Darlington.
Stockton 4/6/50.
Borough Gardens 8/6/58.
York 14/6/59.
Blaydon 1/11/59.
Consett 6/5/62.
South Blyth 16/6/63.
York 8/9/63.
North Blyth 21/8/66.
Tyne Dock 5/3/67.

CONDEMNED: 2/8/67.
Sold for scrap to Hughes,
Bolckow, Blyth 9/67.

62061

N.B.L. Co. 26665.

To traffic 27/12/1949.

REPAIRS:
Dar. 1—7/8/51.**C/L.**
Don. 1—28/5/52.**G.**
Dar. 25—29/7/54.**C/L.**
Don. 21/9—18/10/54.**G.**
Don. 15/12/55—11/1/56.**C/L.**
Don. 6/9—11/10/57.**G.**
Don. 11/3—8/4/61.**G.**

BOILERS:
10720.
29713 (ex62058) 28/5/52.
29717 (ex62057) 18/10/54.
29756 (ex62053) 11/10/57.
29692 (ex62032) 8/4/61.

All seventy began with, and retained, red, cream and grey lining on their black paint. Also, they began with the LNER modified 6 and 9 in the cab side numbers and smokebox plate. The first fifty, Nos.62001 to 62050 carried BRITISH RAILWAYS on the tender. The last twenty, beginning with 62051 on 3rd November 1949, had the 28 inch size emblem instead of lettering.

At their first repair and repainting, Nos.62001 to 62050 had BRITISH RAILWAYS replaced by the emblem, and changed to correct Gill sans 6 and 9 on the cab side.

The only subsequent livery alteration was change of emblem to BR crest from mid-1957 duly effective on all seventy. Like all the other classes to gain the BR crest, the K1's at first had the heraldically wrong crest on the right hand side but all were eventually changed to the correct version.

When Doncaster ceased to repair steam locomotives in the November of 1963, maintenance moved to Darlington and No.62065, ex works 2nd May 1964 carried electrification warning signs. Final repairs were done by Cowlairs - 62044 ex works 16th May 1966 and 62059 out 22nd September 1966 after casual/heavy repairs.

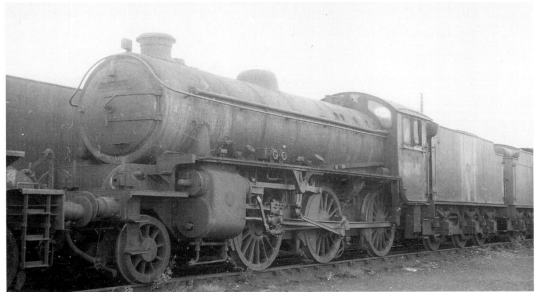

The general change-over to diesel traction led to considerable neglect of the surviving members of K1 class. Withdrawals began with two Fort William engines, Nos.62034 and 62052 on 29th December 1962 but was not completed until the 30th December 1967 with No.62005 as the last of the class.

62001 spent all its working life in the North Eastern Region. It began work at Darlington but moved to Stockton 4th June 1950, from where it was working this goods train. Back to Darlington 4th November 1951 until 14th September 1958 when it went again to Stockton. Thornaby got it on 14th June 1959 until 7th April 1963 when it once again went back to Darlington. Three years later it went to West Hartlepool on 27th March 1966 and from there to York on 5th February 1967 where it ended its days on 25th April of the same year.

62039, working from March shed, was a most unusual sight coasting down Stoke bank into Grantham carrying G.E. discs to show type of train.

SHEDS:
Darlington.
Haverton Hill 7/10/51.
York 10/6/56.

CONDEMNED: 14/12/64.
Sold for scrap to A.Draper, Hull, 2/65. Cut up 1/3/65.

62062

N.B.L. Co. 26666.

To traffic 9/1/1950.

REPAIRS:
Dar. 17—24/11/51.**C/L.**
Don. 11/6—11/7/52.**G.**
Don. 17/8—20/9/54.**G.**
Don. 19/8—14/9/55.**N/C.**
Don. 9—13/4/56.**C/L.**
Don. 12/11—6/12/57.**G.**
Don. 21/7—24/8/60.**G.**
Don. 5—29/11/62.**C/H.**
Dar. 27/5—15/8/64.**G.**
Dar. 17—20/8/64.**N/C.**

BOILERS:
10721.
10721 reno.29721 24/11/51.

29723 *(ex62045)* 11/7/52.
29716 *(ex62046)* 20/9/54.
29695 *(ex62065)* 6/12/57.
29740 *(ex62052)* 24/8/60.

SHEDS:
Darlington.
York 10/6/56.
Darlington 1/11/59.
York 18/8/63.
North Blyth 21/8/66.

CONDEMNED: 24/5/67.
Sold for scrap to Hughes, Bolckow, Blyth 8/67.

62063

N.B.L. Co. 26667.

To traffic 13/1/1950.

REPAIRS:
Dar. 9—16/8/50.**C/L.**
Dar. 13—20/11/51.**C/L.**
Don. 17/9—15/10/52.**G.**
Don. 16/6—13/7/54.**C/L.**
Don. 7/3—1/4/55.**G.**
Don. 21—25/2/56.**C/L.**
Don. 15—19/11/56.**C/L.**

Don. 24/10—19/11/57.**G.**
Don. 28/6—29/7/60.**G.**
Don. 12/11—7/12/62.**C/H.**

BOILERS:
10722.
10722 reno.29722 20/11/51.
29687 *(ex62028)* 15/10/52.
29694 *(ex62030)* 1/4/55.
29704 *(ex62006)* 19/11/57.
29721 *(ex62024)* 29/7/60.

SHEDS:
Darlington.
Stockton 25/6/50.
Darlington 4/11/51.
York 10/6/56.

CONDEMNED: 7/9/64.
Sold for scrap to A.Draper, Hull, 11/64. Cut up 23/11/64.

62064

N.B.L. Co. 26668.

To traffic 19/1/1950.

REPAIRS:
Dar. 28/9—5/10/51.**C/L.**

Don. 17/7—15/8/52.**G.**
Dar. 18—22/9/54.**C/L.**
Don. 16/12/54—8/1/55.**C/L.**
Don. 15/2—15/3/56.**G.**
Don. 23/8—7/9/57.**C/H.**
Don. 7/5—6/6/59.**G.**
Don. 2/4—9/5/62.**G.**
Don. 10/12/62—3/1/63.**C/H.**

BOILERS:
10723.
10723 reno.29720 5/10/51.
29748 *(ex??)* 15/8/52.
29724 *(ex62065)* 15/3/56.
29697 *(ex62014)* 7/9/57.
29707 *(ex62027)* 6/6/59.
29687 *(ex62043)* 9/5/62.

SHEDS:
Darlington.
Stockton 25/6/50.
Darlington 8/6/58.

CONDEMNED: 13/9/65.
Sold for scrap to ?? 10/65.

WORKS CODES:- Cw - Cowlairs. Dar- Darlington. Dfu - Dunfermline shed. Don - Doncaster. Etfd - Eastfied shed. Ghd - Gateshead. Gor - Gorton. Inv - Inverurie.
ThJ - Thornton Junction shed. Str - Stratford. VcA - Vickers Armstrong.
REPAIR CODES:- **C/H** - Casual Heavy. **C/L** - Casual Light. **G** - General. **H**- Heavy. **H/I** - Heavy Intermediate. **L** - Light. **L/I** - Light Intermediate. **N/C** - Non-Classified.

92

62065

N.B.L. Co. 26669.

To traffic 23/1/1950.

REPAIRS:
Dar. 6—9/2/51.**C/L.**
Dar. 1—6/9/51.**C/L.**
Don. 11/8—5/9/52.**G.**
Dar. 11—19/10/54.**C/L.**
Don. 25/5—16/6/55.**C/L.**
Don. 30/6—6/7/55.**N/C.**
Don. 30/12/55—23/1/56.**C/H.**
Don. 29/10—27/11/57.**G.**
Don. 9—14/2/59.**C/L.**
Don. 23/8—7/10/60.**G.**
Dar. 6/12/63—2/5/64.**G.**
Dar. 21/12/64—22/1/65.**C/L.**

BOILERS:
10724.
10724 reno.29715 6/9/51.
29724 *(ex62056)* 5/9/52.
29695 *(ex62040)* 23/1/56.
29724 *(ex62064)* 27/11/57.
29720 *(ex62029)* 7/10/60.
29712 *(ex62060)* 2/5/64.

SHEDS:
Darlington.
Stockton 25/6/50.
Low Moor 14/6/59.
York 30/8/59.

CONDEMNED: 20/3/67.
Sold for scrap to A.Draper,
Hull, 4/7/67. Cut up 28/8/67.

62066

N.B.L. Co. 26670.

To traffic 27/1/1950.

REPAIRS:
Don. 23/1—15/2/52.**G.**
Don. 7/4—6/5/54.**G.**
Don. 9—19/5/55.**C/L.**
Don. 4—13/10/55.**C/L.**
Don. 17/5—15/6/56.**G.**
Don. 24—27/4/57.**N/C.**
Don. 16—21/9/57.**C/L.**
Don. 11/7—12/8/58.**G.**
Don. 17/9—1/10/59.**C/L.**
Don. 6—10/5/60.**N/C.**
Str. 24—29/7/60.**C/L.**
Don. 26/10—26/11/60.**G.**
Don. 5/10—8/11/62.**C/H.**
Don. 3—22/1/63.**N/C.**

BOILERS:
10725.
29681 *(ex62017)* 15/2/52.

29683 *(ex62013)* 6/4/54.
29682 *(ex62043)* 15/6/56.
29708 *(ex62059)* 12/8/58.
29688 *(ex62016)* 26/11/60.

SHEDS:
March.
Doncaster 11/3/62.

CONDEMNED: 10/1/65.
Sold for scrap to A.Draper,
Hull, 2/65. Cut up 29/5/65.

62067

N.B.L. Co. 26671.

To traffic 1/2/1950.

REPAIRS:
Don. 20/4—18/5/51.**G.**
Don. 27/1—21/2/53.**G.**
Don. 22/3—2/4/54.**N/C.**
Don. 19—31/8/54.**C/L.**
Don. 14/1—11/2/55.**G.**
Don. 15/2—7/3/56.**C/L.**
Don. 20/9—2/10/56.**C/L.**
Don. 27/12/56—17/1/57.**C/L.**
Don. 30/1—21/2/58.**G.**
Don. 24/8—5/10/60.**G.**
Don. 24/10—18/11/60.**C/L.**
Don. 28/5—12/7/63.**G.**
Dar. 8/4—8/5/64.**C/L.**
Dar. 3/11—20/12/65.**C/H.**
Cow. ?/?—?/5/66.**?.**

BOILERS:
10726.
29688 *(ex62029)* 21/2/53.
29741 *(ex62048)* 11/2/55.
29709 *(ex62009)* 21/2/58.
29684 *(ex62023)* 12/7/63.

SHEDS:
March.
Retford 27/5/62.
Frodingham 10/1/65.
North Blyth 10/10/65.

CONDEMNED: 18/1/67.
Sold for scrap to A.Willoughby,
Choppington, 17/3/67.

62068

N.B.L. Co. 26672.

To traffic 14/2/1950.

REPAIRS:
Don. 31/1—27/2/52.**G.**
Don. 5/3—1/4/54.**G.**
Don. 21/10—2/11/54.**C/L.**
Don. 5—21/4/55.**C/H.**

Don. 25/5—4/7/56.**G.**
Don. 22/2—2/3/57.**C/L.**
Don. 8—12/4/57.**C/L.**
Don. 23/12/57—2/1/58.**C/L.**
Don. 3—14/5/58.**C/L.**
Don. 30/9—1/11/58.**G.**
Don. 8/10—10/11/60.**G.**
Don. 20/1—7/2/61.**C/L.**
Don. 27/11—18/12/62.**C/H.**

BOILERS:
10727.
29704 *(ex62001)* 1/4/54.
29750 *(ex62039)* 21/4/55.
29739 *(ex62035)* 4/7/56.
29710 *(ex62069)* 1/11/58.

SHEDS:
March.
Doncaster 11/3/62.

CONDEMNED: 18/1/64.
Into Don. for cut up 13/2/64.

62069

N.B.L. Co. 26673.

To traffic 20/2/1950.

REPAIRS:
Don. 25/2—19/3/52.**G.**
Don. 23/2—23/3/54.**G.**
Don. 10—14/5/54.**N/C.**
Don. 10—22/12/54.**C/L.**
Don. 24/4—26/5/56.**G.**
Don. 24/5—1/6/57.**C/L.**
Don. 4/6—11/7/58.**G.**
Don. 13/4—12/5/60.**G.**
Don. 7—30/11/62.**C/H.**

BOILERS:
10728.
29711 *(ex62009)* 19/3/52.
29733 *(ex62070)* 23/3/54.
29710 *(ex62029)* 26/5/56.
29684 *(ex61997)* 11/7/58.
29743 *(ex62028)* 12/5/60.

SHEDS:
March.
Doncaster 1/1/61.

CONDEMNED: 21/1/64.
Into Don. for cut up 14/2/64.

62070

N.B.L. Co. 26674.

To traffic 29/3/1950.

REPAIRS:
Don. 28/11—21/12/51.**G.**

Don. 22—30/4/52.**N/C.**
Don. 11/2—8/3/54.**G.**
Don. 5—14/5/54.**C/L.**
Don. 14—24/9/54.**C/L.**
Don. 10—26/11/54.**C/L.**
Don. 19/4—23/5/56.**G.**
Don. 7—18/6/56.**N/C.**
Don. 1/4—2/5/58.**G.**
Don. 15/8—22/9/61.**G.**
Don. 28/11—18/12/62.**C/L.**

BOILERS:
10729.
29680 *(ex62019)* 8/3/54.
29721 *(ex62013)* 23/5/56.
29726 *(ex62019)* 2/5/58.
29742 *(ex62051)* 22/9/61.

SHEDS:
March.
Stratford 14/9/58.
March 21/9/58.
Stratford 14/6/59.
March 10/9/61.
Retford 10/6/62.

CONDEMNED: 10/1/65.
Sold for scrap to A.Draper,
Hull, 2/65. Cut up 29/5/65.

62004, new 10th June 1949, like all the class, was delivered to Eastfield shed and run-in by that depot before it went south to Darlington. Here on 19th June 1949 it is passing Eastfield shed on a goods turn.

62040, new 3rd October 1949, worked from March until 8th October 1961 as here on a Class A goods for Whitemoor marshalling yard. It then moved to Retford, and on 4th November 1962 to Doncaster from where it was withdrawn 10th January 1965.